Codebreaking our Future

'To many, the future, or at least most of it, is by definition unknowable. Michael Lee argues that this is not so. The law of cause and effect is universal and because time and space are connected we can know what is yet to come much better than we think. Moreover, grasping this and applying it will make resolving problems that now seem to defy solution easier and will make our future better. *Codebreaking our Future* is an exhaustive study into why we can understand the future and how to do it.'

John F. Copper, Stanley J. Buckman Professor of International Studies (emeritus), Rhodes College, Memphis, TN, and author of more than thirty books

'This is one of those few, wonderful books where you can imagine yourself at the dinner table debating the premise and conclusions of a fascinating theory. Do you come to mutual agreement? Not on your life. Would you invite the guy to dinner again? You bet! *Codebreaking our Future* is a significant book. Not to be missed.'

Peg Kay, President Emeritus, Washington Academy of Sciences

'*Codebreaking our Future* is a decisive global reference work for futurists of different persuasions. Based on the theory of causation, spatio-temporal relations and the cycle theory ubiquitous in the universe, the author has created with great courage his own unique logic and model, FutureFinder, including a practical future monitoring system. The question is, as an assumption of the model, whether the future of the human being pre-exists.'

Zhouying JIN, Professor, Chinese Academy of Social Sciences, and Director, Centre for Technology Innovation and Strategic Studies (CTISS)

'In *Codebreaking our Future*, Michael Lee issues a deceptively and provocatively simple declaration: that the future is caused and therefore knowable. A caused future, he reasons, may be understood through causal models. Grounding his ideas in the wisdom of Aristotle, Aquinas, Kant, Hume, and even Stephen Wolfram, Lee decodes the process of finding the future for individuals, organizations, and nations alike.'

Cynthia G. Wagner, editor, *The Futurist*, World Future Society

'In a sweeping revitalisation of Enlightenment philosophy and science, emphasising natural order and a never-ending chain of causation in the world, Michael Lee explores the relevance of a mechanistic worldview to our ability to foreknow the future. According to Lee, the future does have a hidden nature, and it can be modeled and can largely be controlled. Exploring economic and demographic cycles in history, Lee boldly predicts that "… the greatest crisis of the twenty-first century will not be climate change or Peak Oil, but population decline". For Lee, the stakes of not using the advances of science are high: science can save the world from ideological conflict and is nothing less than "… the hope of nations in this century". Whether you want to place your faith in the salvific properties of science and its ability to instill a sure hope or not, this book is a must read for all working on the possibilities and limits of science in dealing with the future of the planet and its inhabitants.'

Professor Martin de Wit, School of Public Leadership, University of Stellenbosch

'An essential characteristic of great business leaders is to find growth opportunities where no-one else has. This is half of the task. The other half is convincing others to follow. This book summarises Michael Lee's philosophy and vision. They have been shaped by reading widely and reinterpreting canonical thinkers. He strongly argues it is possible to identify and influence the causal forces that shape our future. But his philosophy is also pragmatic and informed by a wealth of business acumen, as is demonstrated by his success at guiding an international industry organisation through good and difficult times. As such, what he calls the FutureFinder model aims to enable other business leaders (present and future) to guide their own organisations to decode and shape a purposeful future.'

Bernardo Batiz-Lazo, FRHistS, Professor of Business History and Bank Management, Bangor University

'Future thinking will no longer be considered an obscure domain for woolly academics. Michael Lee formulates in such a logical way the cause-and-effect relationship resulting in change that it is almost unreal that we didn't find the code earlier. *Codebreaking our Future* is a must read for anyone sceptical about how we can understand and prepare for the future.'

Kaat Exterbille, futurist and transformation consultant, CEO Kate Thomas & Kleyn, Brussels

Codebreaking our Future

Deciphering the future's hidden order

By Michael Lee

infiniteideas

First published in 2014 by
Infinite Ideas Limited
36 St Giles
Oxford
OX1 3LD
United Kingdom

www.infideas.com

A CIP catalogue record for this book is available from the British Library

ISBN 978–1–908984–26–5

Brand and product names are trademarks or registered trademarks of their respective owners.

Cover designed by GRID

Typeset by KerryPress

Printed in Spain

In the Republic of South Africa only, Positive Destiny, in class 41 in the name of Institute of Futurology NPC, will be the recognised sole distributor of this book in accordance with a publishing agreement with Infinite Ideas, Ltd.

*Dedicated to visionaries compelled by
the world's hidden wonders*

'The universe is comprehensible because it is governed by scientific laws; that is to say, its behaviour can be modelled.'

Stephen Hawking, *The Grand Design* (2010)

'We can attempt to understand the present, for the future will inevitably retain compelling aspects of what now exists. And the present, in turn, is profoundly a product of the past.'

John Kenneth Galbraith,
***A History of Economics – The Past as the Present* (1991)**

'The fact that nature lends itself to a description in terms of causal laws suggests the conception that reason controls the happenings of nature.'

Hans Reichenbach,
***The Rise of Scientific Philosophy* (1951)**

'All the effects of nature are only mathematical results of a small number of immutable laws.'

Pierre-Simon Laplace,
***Essai philosophique sur les probabilités* (1814)**

'Nothing happens by blind chance.'

Immanuel Kant, *Critique of Pure Reason* (1781)

'It is rightly laid down that true knowledge is that which is deduced from causes.'

Francis Bacon, *Novum Organum* (1620)

'The vapour drawn up from the earth is bound to cool down; once it has cooled down it is bound to turn to rain and fall back to earth.'

Aristotle, *Physics* (c. 350 BC)

Contents

List of figures

List of tables

Foreword

Can the code in which the future is written be deciphered, or will its meaning remain forever out of reach, incomprehensible to the human mind? Just as Egyptian hieroglyphs once looked meaningless to mystified European eyes, the changes happening everywhere in the world seem, on the surface at least, to make little sense. They appear to offer only tantalising hints of what they might signify.

But under the surface, there is structure. Beyond the change, there is causation. Behind the events, nature's laws are secretly, ceaselessly, at work. The signs of our times can be read once their significance is understood. Just as the ancient hieroglyphs turned out to be comprehensible in the end, the language of the future will be decoded.

In a groundbreaking act of intellectual detective work in Paris in 1822, Jean-François Champollion, steeped in knowledge of ancient Egypt, deciphered the Rosetta Stone and unlocked the meaning of its hieroglyphics. Breaking the code of this long-lost language opened the way for the rediscovery of Egypt's great past civilisation. Battling an array of physical ailments and controversy, Champollion went on to become the founding father of Egyptology. The Rosetta Stone itself has since become the most visited object in the British Museum.

The content of the engraved words on the Rosetta Stone, which was discovered by Napoleon's army in 1799 during the French Campaign in Egypt and Syria, is not important. It's simply a boring official decree issued in 196 BC at Memphis, in the Nile Delta, for King Ptolemy V.

Figure 1: The Rosetta Stone (image © Vladimir Korostyshevskiy/123RF.com)

What's important is that the decree appeared in three scripts: Egyptian hieroglyphs, Demotic script and Ancient Greek. This fact allowed Champollion to compare unknown hieroglyphs with the corresponding known words from the other languages on the stone in order to work out their hidden meaning and, more importantly, to deduce the principles of the hieroglyphs. He concluded that they formed a complex written system made up mostly of ideograms (picture words) and phonetic signs (where a character signifies a sound). He also noticed that there were 1,419 hieroglyphs on the Rosetta Stone for only 486 Greek words, indicating that the former had to contain whole words as well as many signs for parts of words.

Champollion's breakthrough moment came when he deciphered the royal name 'Rameses' in the hieroglyphs. He felt he'd taken hold of a key which could help him decrypt several more hieroglyphs. The code had been broken.

The future, like the hieroglyphs, is scripted in strange-looking signs that only seem to be incomprehensible. But what exactly is the code for reading and understanding the signs and language of the future? More pertinently, is there already enough knowledge of the world to enable us to model the future in ways which will help us to manage it better than we ever dreamed would be possible?

A model of the future, representing properties and processes which produce it, is presented in the following pages. It will be shown that the future has an intelligible character, a hidden order which can be known using scientific methods of investigation. By applying a causal model of the world, we can decode the underlying driving forces of the future's order which is deeply embedded in the reality of the present.

The future speaks to us in the language of change. Change, in turn, has a code that can be cracked. That's because it must abide by the law of causation.

Modern science has deciphered the code for reading reality by unearthing its physical laws and the principles of how its processes work. The future, too, while hidden and somewhat mysterious on the surface, operates according to the same universal forces which we know produce reality on an ongoing basis.

Once he'd broken the code of its written language, Jean-François Champollion was enraptured by what he discovered about Ancient Egypt.

Much, much more interesting, though, are the landscapes, nations, populations and civilisations of the future.

Michael Lee
June 2014, Cape Town

Acknowledgements

Timeless classics of science, from Aristotle's *Physics* to Einstein's *Relativity*, have attempted to discover and describe the hidden order of the world. In addition, major philosophical works have established universal principles of thought and logic. Laws of nature and fundamental facts about the world have been unveiled through a superhuman effort over many centuries by legendary scientists from Copernicus to Stephen Hawking.

To construct the causal model for foreknowledge developed in this work, I drew supporting insights and principles from many of the most amazing and revered books of science and philosophy ever written. These writers and thinkers include Euclid, Aristotle, Aquinas, Copernicus, Galileo, Kepler, Bacon, Descartes, Newton, Laplace, Boole, Euler, Hume, Kant, Hegel, Einstein, Reichenbach and, more recently, Professor Hawking and Dr Stephen Wolfram, author of *A New Kind of Science*.

It was surprising and exhilarating for me, while reading these classical works of human thought, to find that the grounds for a science of foreknowledge have, in fact, been illuminated by so many of the world's greatest minds. Thanks to them, the case for futurology may be demonstrated in these pages well beyond any human doubt. Q.E.D.

On a more personal note, I'd like to pay tribute to the Institute for Futures Research (IFR) at the University of Stellenbosch in Cape Town for pioneering the discipline of futures studies in

South Africa and for awakening a passion in me to understand the future in a systematic way.

At the same time, I owe much to Clem Sunter, South Africa's leading business thinker and scenario strategist. His high road/low road scenarios in the later 1980s and early 1990s helped to create the climate for negotiations to forge the new rainbow nation of South Africa. Besides, on a personal level, his generous and gentlemanly support at the launch of my first book on futurology won't easily be forgotten.

On the global stage, I'd like to put on record my appreciation for the work of the World Future Society which provides a worldwide 'church' for futurists and forward-thinking individuals. Born in the USA during the dangers of the Cold War, WFS has since nurtured tens of thousands of citizens of the future, of which I am only one, over four tireless decades.

Finally, true gratitude is expressed to Nelson Rolihlahla Mandela (1918–2013), who, more than any other leader, gave a new future to my nation as well as to global race relations at a time when that positive future looked impossible to all but the most diehard and resilient of idealists.

1

Codebreaking the future

'Observation informs us about the past and the
present; reason foretells the future.'
**Hans Reichenbach, *The Rise of Scientific
Philosophy* (1951)**

The future is caused and causes never lie.

Causation – what influences things to act – forms the core
of a scientific understanding of the world. Since the future is
formed through causation, it can be understood and known.
That's because the same causal processes which were at
work in the past will produce our future world. By analysing
them, we can decode the future, interpreting the meaning of
what lies ahead. If we can understand the mechanics of future
formation in this way, models of the future can be developed,
and even programmed in software. These models will help us
to manage human destiny for the first time.

We're about to learn how to read the signs of the times.

The happy fact is that the future pre-exists, enabling us to
prefigure – or preconstruct – it. As the magnificent medieval
thinker, Thomas Aquinas, argued as long ago as the thirteenth
century, effects pre-exist in their causes.[1]

Let's say, rather prosaically, I've planned to decorate the TV lounge in our home. I've bought paint and brushes, everything else is ready, including the ladder and the protective sheets to cover furniture or floors, and I'm dressed in old clothes. My wife is looking sceptical. I start to paint. Note, that before I begin, my action was already prefigured and planned. My desire to renovate the room was the primary cause of the event. My vision of how the room will look after it's freshly painted reinforced this desire, causing me to buy the materials and utensils needed to perform the act. The action of painting then causes the room to change appearance, to look brighter and newer.

These effects, once envisioned in my plan when they were still in the future, were prefigured in my mind. I saw them coming. Once the causes were in place – the desire, the vision, the plan, the preparatory steps – the outcome in the future became all but inevitable: a newly painted room to appreciate.

In this way, the future pre-exists as a phase in a long series of causes which began in the past and runs through the present into the future. The future, that is, is formed by a combination of causes which can all usually be identified beforehand. So we can prefigure in the present what is pre-existent about the future.

From the dim, early origins of human thought, philosophers have asked what underlying physical elements lie beneath the surface of never-ending changes. For most of history, the four-element world of earth, air, water and fire, developed by Empedocles in the fifth century BC, reigned supreme. Today we have, not four, but 118 known elements, including 92 found on Earth, and we're still counting. The periodic table which outlines them describes the fundamental properties of each of these vital building blocks of matter. This table is a description of the underlying elements of life arranged in a precise order or sequence. By capturing the atomic essence of the substances of our material world, this masterpiece of chemistry, first produced by Dmitri Mendeleev in 1869, enables us to explain and manage the basic physical processes of nature which were once a mystery to humanity. This example shows how science identifies the underlying periodic, or recurrent, order beneath the surface of changes.

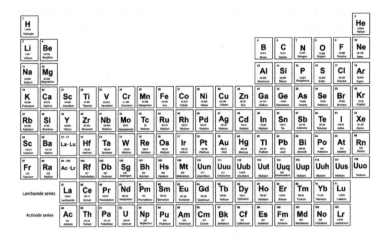

Figure 2: The periodic table of the elements (© jelen80/123RF.com)

It goes without saying that the conceptual order created by the periodic table in Figure 2 doesn't just increase our understanding of the properties of, and relationships between, the elements of the physical universe arranged in their order. It also enables chemists and other scientists to manage the physical processes of life, for example, in the fields of medicine or in the creation of new, improved technologies. The conceptual order of the periodic table leads, inevitably, to greater social order as well as enhanced human well-being. In turn, this enables us to extend our understanding of the physical world even more. Figure 3 illustrates this virtuous circle of increasing order.

The question that springs to mind immediately for me on looking at Figure 3 is this: does the future, too, have an order, one which we can subject to this virtuous circle of science? If it does, then we can conceptualise, model and manage the order of the future just as chemistry uses its priceless periodic table to understand how the elements of the world are composed and how they are related to one another in order.

Another example of this virtuous circle of science is applying the laws and equations of physics, which define the forces of the universe, including gravity and energy, in the fields of aviation, space exploration and nuclear power to extend our technological control over nature. The Standard Model of Particle Physics, for example, is a master equation which explains how three of the major forces that act on matter (excluding gravity) interact with all the particles of matter.

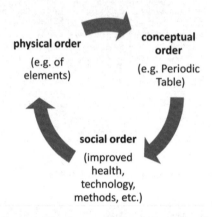

physical order
(e.g. of elements)

conceptual order
(e.g. Periodic Table)

social order
(improved health, technology, methods, etc.)

Figure 3: The virtuous circle of scientific order

Figure 4 shows the essence of this model fitting onto the side of a coffee mug. But this is not all. From cosmology to biology, sciences have identified and traced the origins and long-term developmental processes of life and matter. We've discovered how solar systems, galaxies, stars, organisms, societies and even civilisations have evolved over extended periods of time. We've observed lifecycles and patterns and principles of development at work across different timescales in all these phenomena. Things evolve according to laws of nature. Einstein rightly believed we live in a causal cosmos, one operating according to laws and principles known to reason.

A causal cosmos must give rise to a caused future. A caused future, in turn, is one which may be understood by using a proper causal model.

Evidence will be shared that many of the processes of life occur automatically, according to a built-in design, indicating that the future itself may even be predesigned. It evolves according to templates built into the known fabric of matter and life. The most obvious example of a predetermined biological template is DNA. Nature largely lives, grows and develops through the materialisation of its DNA codes.

Figure 4: Putting the laws of nature into a master formula

Consider, for a moment, the amazing fact of the conception and growth of human life if you don't believe that the future pre-exists. The starting point of each human being is the zygote. This is a single cell created when a mother's egg is fertilised. Despite being truly miniscule, it contains all the genetic information – the genome – needed to form a whole new person. That is, its unique pattern of chromosomes will determine the genetic characteristics of each individual.

About thirty hours after being fertilised, the zygote, containing this DNA blueprint, begins the self-replicating cell division process called mitosis. The growth of a human being in all its complexity is under way. The development follows the built-in plan programmed in the zygote.

At conception, then, each person's future growth is contained inside a code compacted into a cell so tiny it can only be measured on a micrometre scale. The future is already in the egg.

Although the zygote is not conscious during its operations and activities, intelligence is clearly at work. The cell processes a significant amount of information, determining which steps will be followed in the right sequence at the right times. For that reason some have called the nucleus of the zygote an information centre: it stores its own instruction manual, nothing less than a programme for producing a person. The fact that DNA, a key defining feature of life, is a code says something fundamental about the way existence has been made. Since all physical life is coded in this way, it shouldn't be so strange for us to discover that the future, too, has its own code.

What's intriguing is that the individual's genome, embedded in the zygote, seems to switch on and work automatically. Like a computer programme, it contains instructions or rules which control a process of execution. To produce a human being, it's estimated there must be millions of rules involved.[2]

The story of how the zygote works shows that much of human life is biologically predetermined according to a blueprint. As we've seen, the future adult is contained within a code inside a cell. And its evolution in the material world is automatic, or programmed. Other humans have minimal influence over the processes of its development. The individual's future is slowly unlocked according to instructions of a conception blueprint. Life is definitely coded.

It's not just the genome in our DNA-packed zygote in Figure 5 which determined who we would become, eventually made up from approximately 40,000 genes.[3] We don't get to choose our parents or the genealogy they bring with them in the history stored in their genes. Neither do we select our place and time of birth. Similarly, we choose neither our siblings nor how we are brought up and educated. Our conception, birth and growth are automatic processes. I think this is what Kant meant when he exclaimed: 'I am conscious of my own existence as determined in time.'[4]

And far from being an exceptional occurrence, the way in which each human blueprint runs its programme code for the creation of a new individual is typical of a whole range of automated processes operated by nature's invisible software. It seems science is on a journey to discover a cosmic instruction manual. And the invention of computerisation has greatly accelerated the pace of that discovery.

For example, scientist and creator of Mathematica,[5] Stephen Wolfram, in his monumental *A New Kind of Science* (2002), argues that we live in a digital, mathematical universe. It works on the basis of simple and universal computational programmes producing very complex natural systems. He describes in plain language how 'our universe is in essence just a simple program' with 'a single, simple, underlying rule'.[6] In his theory of simple programmes, there's an upper limit or ceiling to complexity and to computational sophistication.[7] Back in 1814, Pierre-Simon Laplace wrote an influential essay called *Essai philosophique sur les probabilités* in which he claimed: 'All the effects of nature are only mathematical results of a small number of immutable laws.'[8] Wolfram and Laplace both saw evidence displayed throughout the universe of a mathematical order at work.

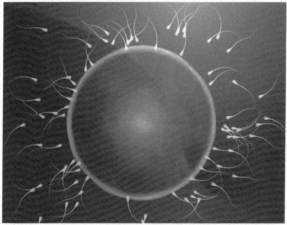

Figure 5: The human zygote containing a person's genome
(© Can Stock Photo Inc./kgtoh)

Wolfram urges us to think in terms of these simple programmes to understand how nature works: 'just as the rules for any system can be viewed as corresponding to a programme, so also its behaviour can be viewed as corresponding to a computation ... all processes, whether they are produced by human effort or occur spontaneously in nature, can be viewed as computations ... set up specifically to perform particular tasks'.[9] Computations calculate according to rules or instructions for set tasks and functions. In Wolfram's worldview, a simple universal order underlies all of nature's complex design. Nature has a rule book. Like human life, it's coded. Its archetypal designs are programmed: 'the basic mechanisms responsible for many processes in nature can be captured by simple computer programs based on simple rules'.[10]

Nature, then, runs on a predetermined built-in programme. For example, Wolfram shows that determining the huge variety of shapes of trees and leaves is a straightforward branching process during growth. In 1808, Alexander von Humboldt identified nineteen types of this underlying branching phenomenon.[11] Likewise, a few basic patterns underlie the diversity of appearances of animals. There is substantial uniformity across nature. And the processes underlying it are automated and intelligent.

Is there a similar intelligent order of the future which is coded into existence?

If everything that happens in the world operates like the execution of an underlying programme and its rules, just as the zygote unlocks the growth of an individual according to its blueprint, perhaps the future itself can be deciphered, read and foreseen. Its elements could be allocated in a 'periodic table' of the future.

Amassing colossal evidence from the behaviour of computer programmes and natural systems, including biological ones, Wolfram has revealed a self-organising, 'all is computation', universe. He's demonstrated great similarities between mathematics and nature. We're dealing with an intelligent universe in which the laws of physics show 'computational sophistication'.[12]

The future, likewise, should be intelligent rather than blind. Kant himself was convinced that nothing happens in the world by chance. In that case, the future cannot emerge by chance. Rather, it's as highly structured as the rest of reality.

Can we learn to automate the future? Computer programmes which forecast the future have already been developed, as will be seen later in this book. Processes in nature do seem to be set up to run automatically according to an instruction manual. In such a causal, self-organised world, why wouldn't there be an order behind the future?

The coded nature of existence strengthens the idea of knowing the future. Know the programme and you know its future outcomes. If there's so much that's recurrent or periodic in nature, with so many of its processes automatic and apparently preprogrammed, it's natural to conclude that the future will closely resemble the past in its underlying patterns and structure.

Furthermore, everything has a purpose and a function for which it exists. A vast array of thinkers have noticed how things strive to fulfil the purposes and functions of their existence. Evolution itself shows just how goal-directed and purpose-driven existence is. It points, like time, in the direction of the future: the sphere of predesigned development.

If these purposes, or goals, are implanted in living things as part of the very form of their existence, it follows that their future destiny is pre-existent. Their future, that is, is designed into life, just as the example of the genome package within the human zygote shows.

In addition to biological DNA templates driving existence like this, there are also mental causes of life arising from within the psyche of living beings. Actions may result from visions or ideas which Aquinas called exemplars: 'an idea is an exemplar insofar as an idea is the source in producing things, and ideas as exemplars belong to practical knowledge'.[13] We'll return to these kinds of internal causes of the future later in describing our causal model of the future.

Modern science, then, has comprehensively mapped out the fundamental substances and forces underpinning the workings of the world. The ancient philosophical question of how things behave with regularity, despite constant change, has been answered. Together, the periodic table, the laws of motion, gravity and energy, genomics and the Standard Model of Particle Physics show that change is underwritten by order. This known order extends from the tiniest atomic structure of the elements of the periodic table out to the sublime vastness of the cosmos.

It also extends into the future world.

Specifically, what science shows us is that a golden chain of causation runs right through the universe, time, Earth, human nature, society and knowledge. This chain of causation is, without question, the backbone of knowledge,[14] including knowledge of the future. As Kant has stated, 'Causality leads us to the concept of action; that of action to the concept of force; and, through it, to the concept of substance.'[15]

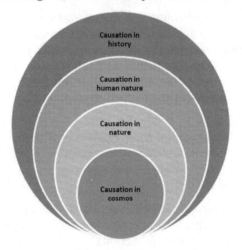

Figure 6: The golden chain of causation

Science's treasure chest of knowledge is built around this core concept of causation. And social sciences, such as history, politics, economics, demography and sociology, have employed scientific methods to construct expansive theories of how societies, population groups and economies function and develop according to universal patterns. Meanwhile, systems thinking has outlined how to analyse all natural and social systems within one framework of systems behaviour. This phenomenal body of scientific, philosophical, social and historical knowledge can now be harnessed to understand the future before it happens.

In this book a model of the future is constructed using the latest scientific, philosophical, social and historical knowledge. In particular, a code for reading our common future will be presented which contains a range of indicators evaluating known influences impacting change according to observable and regular processes. These causes of coming changes can be outlined and compared, like elements in the periodic table. In this way, knowledge of the future can be pieced together in advance of it coming to pass. Using causal modelling in a systematic way, the ancient inbred art of human anticipation will slowly evolve into a much-needed scientific discipline.

In Chapters 11 to 13, a modelling system called FutureFinder is introduced which sets out the influences on our human future in the order of their importance. Just as the periodic table arranges the known chemical elements into an order so that their properties and interactions can be compared and predicted, so FutureFinder lists the influences on social change to find the causal driving forces of the future for societies, organisations and individuals.

One thing's for sure: whatever lies ahead for the world certainly won't happen in a vacuum. It's impossible for the future to emerge from nowhere. It's a myth to think it can materialise out of thin air.

On the contrary, there's an observable, and largely predictable, set of processes by which the *becoming* of all reality occurs – and has occurred since the beginning of time. Things *become* in a successive evolution, over a continuous time frame, and all in accordance with laws of nature and development.

The future is produced. It emerges in a systemic, mechanical and, at times, automatic way. If the elements and forces underpinning change in the universe have been modelled, why can't we model the systemic changes that will produce our common future?

As the range of influences which cause change are studied, the code of the future is gradually deciphered. A system of mapping and measuring its causes can be developed based on which influences are at work in the continuous process of becoming. The future would no longer be considered a realm of obscurity beyond the laws of nature. It would no longer be viewed as a domain of mystery which is 'above the law'.

On the contrary, the future must conform to laws, not just the laws of natural and social evolution but the laws of time built into reality. These laws of time are explained in Chapter 4.

In this generation, the future should largely cease to be a mystery. That's not a prediction but a pre-fact – that is, a fact known ahead of its materialisation in the world. On a mass scale, the future's hieroglyphics of surface uncertainty will be understood by applying the underlying code of the future. When Champollion cracked the code of the hieroglyphs on the Rosetta Stone in 1822, the future creation of Egyptology became inevitable, a reality unlocked from time by a determined codebreaker.

Seen in simple terms, the future is the forward direction of space–time, the medium in which all life exists. And science has a body of proven knowledge about how our space–time works. As Stephen Hawking wrote in the introduction to his history of mathematics: 'the greatest wonder of the modern world is our own understanding'.[16] I agree; the sum of what we know now about the universe is immense. Despite this knowledge, we often choose to wallow in uncertainty, especially regarding the future.

The future cannot be outside the reach of science and logic.

Since our future is made up of the next phases of our world of space–time, and since we understand the laws and principles underpinning space–time, how can the future be incomprehensible or inconceivable? The future isn't some sort of Never-Never Land beyond our mental powers of reason and observation.

Needless to say, the code of the future has nothing to do with fortune-telling, astrology or gazing into a crystal ball. Rather, it's about extending the methods of science to study what lies in front of us in time. It's about observing what our space–time world is in the process of becoming. In the coming years, through science, we'll improve our capacity for looking into the future a thousandfold.

But, before we get there, let's define the purpose of foreseeing the future. The reasons for modelling and managing the future turn out to be irresistible.

2

Managing the future

'The only immediate utility of all sciences is to teach us how to control and regulate future events by their causes.'

David Hume, *An Enquiry Concerning Human Understanding* (1748)

In this evocative statement, Hume urges humanity to regulate the future based on an understanding of how causes produce events. The future cannot be managed without foreknowledge gained by studying causes. This kind of foreknowledge may be used to change direction if need be so we're always moving in the right direction – that is, towards sustainable, long-term advancement.

As a believer in futurology, it's a dream that every person, organisation and society in the world should become proactive, fully conscious of the power to better control the future in the way Hume assumed was possible.

Since our civilisation is committed to progress, it makes sense to gain a stronger grip on the handle of future events.

At this time, however, human progress is still shrouded in immense uncertainty. For example, the previous century was characterised by unprecedented achievements in technological advancement while, at the same time, staging history's bloodiest and most horrifying conflicts. Something must be wrong, badly wrong, with our idea of progress. Otherwise, such a glaring dichotomy between barbaric behaviour and material advances would never have happened in this way.

There are two possible problems with our approach to managing the future which might explain why the twentieth century was so conflicted and violent in the midst of this unparalleled development of technology, including in aviation, space exploration, computerisation and mobile communications.

First, societies have adopted ideological approaches to policy making, whether capitalistic, communistic or something in-between. Ideology has proven to be a disastrous construct for management of society. An ideology-neutral scientific perspective on the future would be far less toxic.[17]

The second drawback which has held back the regulation of the future, using Hume's terms, is that change travels faster than knowledge. As a futurist and eternal student, I'd love knowledge to travel faster than the speed of change, but it doesn't. To this day, it's a painfully slow process to accumulate knowledge, especially scholarly knowledge. By contrast, change happens at speeds we often find bewildering, as Alvin Toffler showed so decisively in his 1970 sociological masterpiece *Future Shock*. Consequently, we always seem to be one step behind the forces of change.

However, with the wonders of the internet, whereby information can be digitised and sent around the world in seconds, and with the tools of futurology, we can finally reverse this situation. We're entering a time when the world will produce five billion gigabytes of data on the internet every ten minutes. I'm convinced the speed at which we gain and distribute knowledge will one day outpace the global forces of change. This capacity will make our societies much more ordered and robust.

It's always beneficial to plan ahead, instead of reacting too late to changes which take us – and our systems – by surprise. But we must understand that information needs to be structured within a scientific framework, and evaluated according to logical and philosophical principles, in order to become truly useful. Otherwise, digital data on the kind of scale we see today will lead only to information overload, not to improved strategic planning and certainly not to better regulation of the future.

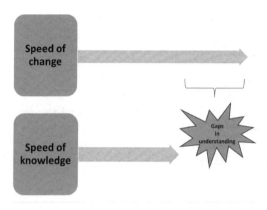

Figure 7: Change outpacing the acquisition of knowledge

Since it's much better to be in control of the process of change rather than to be controlled by it, what do we have to do to stop falling behind change, as illustrated in Figure 7?

The only way to stay ahead of change is through systematic anticipation. Fortunately, looking ahead is already a well-established evolutionary human skill. One purpose of this book is to take the natural art of anticipation and turn it into a systematic science.

To do that, it's necessary to describe the order, or underlying causal structure, of the future. That's the key right there to Hume's regulation of future events. Knowing how the future works will enable us to keep pace with change. Humanity will be better equipped to direct its technologies and systems towards success, orderliness and sustainability.

The very physics of time screams out for us to be proactive, or anticipatory, in this manner. The universe is faced in one time-direction only – towards the future, never backwards into the past. Life evolves forwards only. Time is incredibly dynamic, moving onwards in an expanding universe at very fast speeds. That's why we need to become better at building knowledge of our world, and foreknowledge of tomorrow's world, as fast as possible.

Figure 8: Time always faces forwards

The future needs to be modelled in order to manage it. Only then can we think of starting to control the forces of change. Furthermore, through scientific systems of foresight, knowledge-based civilisations of the grandest order could be built.

It's knowledge of the material world which has enabled humankind to understand and control it, making it more valuable. Knowledge of the future order would result in a diminishment of chaos in the lives of individuals and in the systems of organisations and societies. It would cut down on wrong decisions.

After thousands of years of stop-start, zigzag human development, an epoch of non-stop progression would begin. Chaos, I believe, is the source of all evil. That's because it breeds dysfunctional behaviour and malfunctioning systems. Dysfunctional systems have significant knock-on effects throughout our interconnected world.

The code of the future outlined in this book may be used to commandeer the future in a new, rather belated, conquest of time. While colonising the three-dimensional spatial world, including outer space, as described by sciences like cosmology, physics, geology, geography, biology and chemistry, societies have often failed to foresee the long-term impacts of policies, technologies and systems.

In our limited view of time, humankind has focused on preserving its collective memories in art, culture and history, while mystifying the future, conceiving it throughout the Modern Age, with few exceptions, as more or less unknowable.

Prognostic social thinkers such as Condorcet, Thomas Malthus, W.S. Jevons, H.G. Wells and M. King Hubbert, and futurists such as Herman Kahn, Buckminster Fuller, Pierre Wack and Alvin Toffler, as well as societies like the World Future Society and academic departments like the Institute for Futures Research, kept alive the study of the future. Nevertheless, the overwhelming consensus remained, and still persists, that uncertainty reigns when it comes to predicting the world of tomorrow.

Today, it seems that only the future remains to us as the last Great Unknown. As I write, it's still a largely uncharted domain of mystery and speculation. The language of the future is regarded by most of humanity, and its thought leaders, as written in hieroglyphs.

But we can decipher this hieroglyphic language of the future using causation as the decryption tool. Causation has been accepted in the major works of science and philosophy down the ages as the core of human knowledge. Later, it will be used to unveil the underlying structure, or hidden order, of the future. The causes of the future will be organised into a predictive system. Imagine the power of equipping the evolutionary skill of anticipation with the tools of science? The possibilities for improving social systems and human life in general are simply breathtaking.

Building on how physics, since Einstein, has demystified time, turning it into a physical medium of change within the spatial world, such a futurology would develop methods for studying how phenomena behave in time. Time may be the final frontier of knowledge but it is not above the laws of nature or beyond our powers of comprehension. Let's embark on a scientific expedition into the future. It will prove to be no alien land.

Just as individuals educate themselves to become literate and numerate, the citizens of the future, whose numbers in this century I predict will swell to millions, will need to become more time-literate. Time literacy requires a proper sense of scale, evaluating the behaviour of entities over different time periods, from the short term to the far future. [18] In time literacy, things are placed into their evolutionary context to enable anticipation of their future direction.

Time literacy can empower people. In his celebrated *Long Walk to Freedom* Nelson Mandela wrote: 'One of the first things I did [on Robben Island] was to make a calendar on the wall of my cell. Losing a sense of time is an easy way to lose one's grip and even one's sanity.'[19] Time confers meaning on the world, giving purpose and direction to things.

Greater time literacy will emerge from understanding the main principles of time. The properties of time are described in Chapter 4 but for now we need only consider the direction of time. As Figure 8 above showed, there's only one physical direction of time – forwards. No exertion of human effort, whether creative or destructive, whether heroic or trivial, can change this fundamental fact of existence. That means two things for our future.

First, there's a predetermined direction to all life which points to the promise of perpetual betterment. For convenience, this principle may be called positive determinism. It speaks of an inherently purposeful form of predestination for the automatic, intelligent world we've been talking about so far in this book.

Second, the fixed forwards direction of time guarantees that history must move in waves. Why so? To understand this, the analogy of the wave is revealing. Waves push their energy forwards as far as it can go until it runs out, whereupon they dissolve on the shore or disappear back into deeper ocean waters. In other words, waves have direction but a limited amount of energy.

Likewise, social and historical movements, from empires to ideologies, from civilisations to value systems, from states to fashions and conventions, have limited energy and always exhaust themselves eventually. Like waves, they move forwards with great vigour after they have been conceived and accepted on an increasing scale. At last, for a host of reasons, these waves run out of momentum, returning to the source from which they came, after which new waves are formed to crash and wash against the coast. Like time, history must always move on, usually in new directions but under exactly the same underlying physical conditions. The direction of time cannot be changed. Nor can the laws of nature. We're condemned by time to go forwards.

The direction of time encourages humanity to align itself with its forward movement, always striving to point in the best direction for long-term stability, keeping in step with the deeper principles of time like sustainability, balance and optimisation.

Since we live in a dynamic moving world, one going forwards at an incredible rate, we need anticipation even more than we need memory to survive and thrive as we head for an ideal state of dynamic equilibrium.

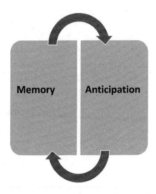

Figure 9: Memory and anticipation balance each other in our minds

While time itself always faces forwards, as a species we tend to face backwards. We invest much more time and energy in understanding the past than we do in preparing for the future. We invest disproportionately more in memory than in anticipation. A proper balance is needed between memory and anticipation.

To manage the future is to manage constant change. It is to be aligned to time. The 'periodic table' of the future – its code – is made up of all different kinds of causes underlying change. If knowledge of the future is scientifically organised, the future can be commandeered. Hume's dream of regulating future events through science will have come closer to realisation.

3

Causing the future

'Present events are connected with preceding ones by a tie based upon the evident principle that a thing cannot occur without a cause which produces it... We ought then to regard the present state of the universe as the effect of its anterior state and as the cause of the one which is to follow... The regularity which astronomy shows us in the movements of the comets doubtless exists also in all phenomena.'

Pierre-Simon Laplace,
A Philosophical Essay on Probabilities **(1814)**

To decode the future is to analyse the total effect of all the influential causes that produce it. The future may be more accurately anticipated by following closely the causes which underlie its processes of change.

In Figure 6, causation was seen as the backbone of scientific knowledge. David Hume stated: 'All reasonings concerning matter of fact seem to be founded on the relation of Cause and Effect.'[20]

Indeed, a never-ending chain of causation does run through the universe, as the above quotation by Laplace also suggests. You only have to think back on the course of your own life to realise it has been made up of countless causes, both internal, arising from within you, and external, arising from the world.

As the backbone of knowledge, this chain of causation is the deciphering tool for interpreting and reading the future's hidden code. It's the future's Rosetta Stone. To enable this tool to be used in practice to decipher the future, a model of causation is developed.

An effective model of causation would contain the following five aspects:

- Argument – an explanation of the philosophy and science of causation.

- Definition – an outline of the elements of causation.

- Taxonomy – a classification of categories of causes.

- Measurement – how to determine the respective influences of various causes.

- Relevance – application of the model for study of the future.

First, then, some explanation about the critical role causation has played in philosophy and science.

Mathematical genius Pierre-Simon Laplace established that every occurrence has a cause which makes it happen. And legendary philosopher Immanuel Kant stated: 'All changes take place according to the law of the connection of Cause and Effect.'[21] The seminal medieval philosopher and theologian, Thomas Aquinas, went so far as to argue that effects actually pre-exist in their causes.

So, 'follow the cause' must be our mantra. If you want to find the future and to manage change, follow the cause. The 'periodic table' of the future will be made up of causes which underlie changes, as illustrated in Figure 10 below.

Just as the periodic table looks below the surface array of apparently unrelated chemical reactions and diverse properties of physical substances to an underlying order of elements, so a causal model will aim to penetrate beyond surface changes to identify a structured network of causes and influences – whether background conditions, underlying dynamics of systems in nature and society or direct causes – which are ultimately responsible for change.

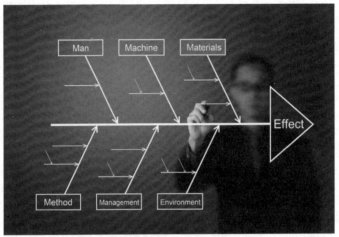

Figure 10: Structure of causal relations underlying changes
(© dskdesign/123RF.com)

In Figure 10, it's easy to spot the contrast between multiple surface activities driving change and their hidden order and structure. Hegel also saw a permanence underlying the surface of nature: 'Nature remains, despite all the contingency of its existence, obedient to eternal laws; but surely this is also true of the realm of self-consciousness, a fact which can already be seen in the belief that providence governs human affairs.'[22]

In searching for the hidden order of the future, the relationship between changes and causes is central. Great minds in philosophy and science have, from time to time, drawn back the veil of this hidden order to reveal what really causes change.

We begin the analysis of causation with a sweeping statement by Thomas Aquinas: 'Everything moved is moved by something else.'[23] Kant agrees: 'everything which happens must have a cause in the appearances of a preceding state'.[24] The great German philosopher called this principle the law of change. He saw a law of causation at work throughout nature: 'according to which an empirically undetermined cause of an event in time cannot exist'.[25] The word 'cannot' here is categorical. For Kant, the law of causation was written in stone, ruling out the possibility of there ever being any uncaused events: 'The natural law, that everything which happens must have a cause, that the causality of this cause, that is, the action of the cause ... must have itself a phenomenal cause, by which it is determined, and, consequently, that all events are empirically determined in an order of nature – this law, I say, which lies at the foundation of the possibility of experience, and of a connected system of appearances or nature, is a law of the understanding, from which no departure, and to which no exception, can be admitted.'[26]

The cornerstone of our model of the future code is this law of causation, so emphatically stated in those timeless words of Kant. That law establishes beyond doubt that all changes and all events are caused. Every event is caused; even acts of free will set in motion a subsequent chain of events and effects and are themselves caused by prior decisions and states. Hume claimed that 'there is nothing existent, either externally or internally, which is not to be considered either as a cause or an effect'.[27]

This marvellous omnipresence of causation ultimately arises from the interdependence of all things in the cosmos. Given such an interdependence of everything, finely articulated, for example, in the Biomatrix theory of systems, it's not at all surprising that everything emerges from something else which precedes it. Parents beget children who, in turn, produce their grandchildren. Summer follows spring; day follows night. Middle age follows youth and, sadly, death occurs to end life. The modern age was preceded by medieval times. Technologies get better all the time, building on previous innovations. And scientific knowledge itself continues to accumulate. The twentieth-century physicist David Bohm called this phenomenon 'antecedence'. His concept speaks of an interactive universe composed of interdependent systems.

Aristotle believed that the process by which something comes from another antecedent thing is causal in nature. A statue may come from bronze. A seed may produce a flower.

A builder builds a house. A pen writes a word, a calculator works out a sum. A conclusion may be drawn from premises. All these outcomes are caused by the entity which enables them to come into being.

The importance of these observations is that the world has a highly causal structure. And its causal processes are largely known to science. In fact, the world is so deeply structured by the laws of nature that it's effectively programmed, as we saw in assessing the science of Stephen Wolfram in Chapter 1.

You can read life by studying its built-in code.

It's the same in understanding the future. The ancients used tea leaves, crystal balls and oracles to read signs of the future. Today, we can read codes through the eyes of science. The code of the future is like source code in a computer. It's written in the language of causation.

The model of causation illustrated in Figure 11 is explained throughout this chapter. The philosophy and science of causation is the right context for understanding the nature, universality and overwhelming importance of causation.

The universal law of causation points, in the view of these major philosophers, to a teleological, or purpose-driven, universe in which everything naturally, unavoidably, strives to reach its inherent purpose: 'the chief efficient cause of any effect strives in the strict sense for what is the final end... But what is best in the world is the good order of the universe.'[28] The law of causation proves that all things are driven and the fact that plans and goals themselves become causes, as we'll see several times in this book, adds to the idea that life is, indeed, inherently purposeful.

The built-in order of cause-and-effect relationships, in which causes have power to change the state of other things, suggests the idea that things tend to fit into a hierarchy of functions, a pecking order, an invisible structure.

Nature, Aquinas argued, 'determines for some things the form by which they act and the end for the sake of which they act, but they move themselves in executing movement... And everything has such a disposition toward its natural form that it strives for the form when it does not possess the form, and is at rest when it possesses the form.'[29] Nature, that is, has an underlying structure of regular relationships which lie behind Aquinas' 'good order of nature', Kant's causal world and Einstein's causal universe.

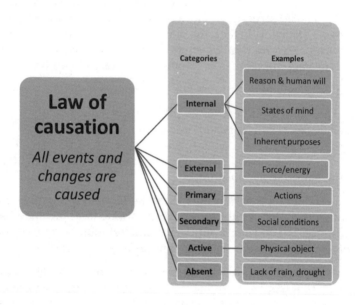

Figure 11: A model of causation

Aristotle's doctrine of causation is based almost entirely on the causative power of the purpose of things, which Aquinas called, in the above excerpt, a natural form: 'So I had better begin by explaining why a thing's nature is a cause in the sense that it has a purpose... Moreover, whenever there is an end, the whole prior sequence of actions is performed with this end as its purpose... But actions have a purpose, and so therefore do things in nature ... since the end is the form, and everything else takes place for the sake of the end, it is this form that is the cause, since it is that for which everything happens ... it is clear that a thing's nature is a cause, and that it is the kind of cause I have been saying – namely, purpose.'[30] The purpose for which things are made becomes a cause of what they do and how they evolve: 'the end is also an originating principle'.[31] A knife is used for cutting, a builder is trained to build, health is the purpose of walking or training. Purposes tend to be causal in that actions and plans are put into effect in order to achieve goals. Aristotle saw purpose everywhere he looked. He knew it was vital for natural scientists to understand the purpose of things and how these purposes drive change in the world.

Figure 10 showed that a causal order underpins all surface change, in keeping with this law, which has an inherent 'feature of necessity'.[32]

Aquinas included human nature, and not just external nature, in his picture of a purpose-driven universe: 'both intellect and nature act for the sake of an end. Therefore, an intellect needs to predetermine the end and the necessary means to the end for causes that act by nature. For example, an archer predetermines the target and path of an arrow. And so a cause acting by intellect and will necessarily precedes a cause acting by nature.'[33] Every efficient cause, he states, 'acts for the sake of an end'.[34]

Causation, then, is often driven by purposes inhering in the functions for which things exist.[35] This is a well-known Aristotelian conception. Each thing has a purpose for which it exists: 'what a thing is and its purpose are the same'.[36] As it happens, the meaning of cause is closely related to the meaning of purpose. In Greek, *aitia* means 'something without which the thing would not be'. The picture here is of a thing striving to fulfil its inherent purpose. In this sense, the purpose 'pulls' a thing into a future in which it can reach its goals, causing a multitude of actions directed at that purpose.

Aristotle was the first major philosopher to develop a systematic description and doctrine of causation. In moving on to an actual definition of causation, it's fitting to begin with this great thinker's views on the topic.

All causes, he said, 'initiate change or stability'.[37] Change, he further claimed, was everlasting, that is, never-ending.[38] There's a sea of constant change all around us. Everything that changes, Aristotle states, 'must be changed by something'.[39]

The first thing one notices about most descriptions of causation is that it's seen as involving some sort of physical exchange between cause and effect: 'There is, then, an immediate agent of change and an object which is being changed.'[40] Aristotle identifies three elements to this exchange: 'there is that which causes change, that which is changed, and the end-point of the change'.[41] Furthermore, the source of change can be outside the changing object or within the changing object itself: 'Some things that are changed in their own right are changed by themselves, while others are changed by external agents.'[42] I'll return to this point later in this chapter.

Causes are agencies of change. They always seem to produce the same, or similar, kinds of effects under normal conditions. 'Constant conjunction', in other words a regular relationship, is a criterion of a cause-and-effect relation according to Hume.[43] He argued that the cause and effect had to be contiguous, in proximity to each other, for this physical influence to take place. In addition, the effect is always subsequent to the cause: 'the two relations of contiguity and succession ...[are] essential to causes and effects'.[44]

Descartes described perfect science as 'knowledge of effects through causes'.[45]

Mellor (1995) explains that causes determine their effects: 'By causes that determine their effects I shall mean ones that are in the circumstances both sufficient and necessary for them. "Sufficient" here means that the existence of the cause ensures ... that its effects also exist. "Necessary" here means that its non-existence ensures ... that its effects do not exist.'[46]

So it seems the cause is superior to the effect in two ways. First, it's ahead in time, or has a temporal advantage. It comes first. Second, it has more productive power. A nail doesn't hit a hammer. A switch doesn't move the hand up and down. Meat can't cook itself.

The exchange we are talking about, which lies at the heart of causation, involves some form of energy from a superior force required to bring about the effect.

Hawking showed that one aspect of time is that it's thermodynamic. It brings about changes in the distribution of energy, with stronger forces affecting and altering weaker ones. In the end, causation is about energy.

Kant defined change as 'transition of a thing from one state to another'.[47] Causes change the conditions, or properties, of things through a redistribution of energy: 'But change is an event, which, as such, is possible only through a cause'.[48] Any effect, he noted, is the necessary consequence of its cause,[49] and by 'necessary' here is meant obeying the laws of nature, especially, we should add, the principles of thermodynamics and energy.[50] He declared that 'every item in the series of events must be subject to rules in such a way that nothing ever occurs without something preceding it and upon which it universally follows'.[51]

Clearly, causes have a relationship of power over their effects, a relationship which is found throughout nature: 'For every cause presupposes a rule, according to which certain appearances follow as effects from the cause, and every rule requires uniformity in these effects; and this is the proper ground of the concept of a cause – as a power.'[52]

Kant describes this causal power as momentum: 'Now every change has a cause, which exhibits its causality in the whole time during which the change takes place... All change is therefore possible only through a continuous action of the causality, which, in so far as it is uniform, we call a momentum. The change does not consist of these momenta, but is produced by them as their effect.'[53] We're looking for the actual energy which produced the effect.

We see causes, then, bringing about changes through their superior power: 'For an efficient cause's power results in the cause imparting to its effect the power to act.'[54] At one point, Hume also uses the word 'power': 'the production of one object by another in any one instance implies a power'.[55] At another point he refers to the 'energy' of causes.[56] I prefer Hume's term because it is, after all, energy that drives all life in its vast, evolutionary struggle, in both nature and society. This crucial exchange of energy, power or momentum means that the cause has to be the physically stronger agent. This is part of the order behind causation. It's also part of the hidden order of the future. Kant argued that 'things are acted upon insofar as they lack something and are imperfect'.[57] It makes sense to speak of the cause being the stronger agent and the effect as the weaker entity. The impact of the exchange of energy can have knock-on effects. Paul and Hall (2003) explain that causes are transitive: if C causes D and D causes E then C causes E.[58]

In sum, let's recap our concept of causation. The simplest way to see it is, in the words of these co-authors, 'A cause brings something about or makes something happen.'[59] Put another way, a cause brings about a change in the state of an effect. In order to achieve that, the cause requires more energy, at the time of the exchange, than the effect. Causation involves an exchange of energy in keeping with physical laws of nature.

Furthermore, there's clearly a chain of causation built into the universe and all its workings. Simply put, causation happens everywhere without ceasing. That's why the concept and doctrine of causation have become so central to both science and philosophy.

It's important to realise that the way causation works shows that nature always obeys its laws: 'Assuming determinism, causes seem also to guarantee the occurrence of their effects.'[60] It's this deterministic way in which causes operate that paves the way for a code of the future. We can read the future because its causes act in incredibly regular and predictable ways.

As a largely material process, causation must be subject to physical laws and principles like everything else.

The third aspect of our model of causation, following its contextualisation and definition above, is an outline of the different categories of causes.

In Figure 11, the following three pairs of categories are set out, making a total of six kinds of cause: internal or external (*source* of cause), primary or secondary (*impact* of cause), active or absent (*occurrence* of cause). Let's define and exemplify each of the six types of cause set out in Figure 11.

- Internal
  These are causes arising within the object or person, such as the purpose or design of a thing, the inner motivation, desire or will of a person, or something's natural limits.

- External
  Here we're referring to forces, objects or systems in the world which exert some physical power or energy over another thing, for example, climate and weather, a tool or instrument, a physical action.

- Primary
  A primary cause is the dominant or most influential and most direct factor producing the effect, for example, a driver falls asleep and loses control of the vehicle which causes a collision. This is sometimes known as the efficient cause because through its activity the effect is actually produced. It's what really caused the change, without which the transaction of causation wouldn't have happened. The primary cause will be responsible for the essential features of the changes measured on the effect(s).

- Secondary
  Secondary causes influence the outcome but not so directly or so energetically as the dominant cause. For example, alcohol or medication caused the drowsiness which led to the driver falling asleep behind the wheel. Or the driver had not slept well leading up to the accident.

- Active
  An active cause is when physical energy of some sort propels the actual causation process through an action, event or activity. For example, a person tells someone else to do something or carries out an action with some consequences.

- Absent
  By contrast to the other half of this pair of causes, an absent cause is when something doesn't happen which normally would, leading to a disruption in the order of things. For example, a lack of rain can cause drought.

When it comes to measuring causation in the next phase of our construction of a model, the role of primary, secondary, active and absent causes will be significant. For the time being, the most important pair for understanding the process by which the future is formed is the distinction between internal and external causes. A cause is internal if it is built into the nature of the thing while it is external if it originates in the application of force or exchange of energy in the outer world.

Regarding internal causes, sometimes called intrinsic causes, the role of human will should not be underestimated. Kant believed man's will 'is the empirical cause of all his actions'.[61] This is a categorical statement showing how important will is to action which, in turn, causes much of what happens in society.

There are, of course, deeper, driving forces of willpower, such as desires, motivations and needs, as well as the influential role reason plays in our decision making. Kant clearly shows how these factors are very much part of the chain of causation we have seen to be the backbone of our knowledge of life. Since these drivers of human behaviour are part of causation, they fall squarely within the scope of scientific enquiry: 'If, then, we could investigate all the appearances of the human will to their very ground, there would be no action which we could not anticipate with certainty, and recognise to be absolutely necessary from its preceding causes.'[62]

Kant is here applying the doctrine of necessity, by which causation is pretty deterministic in how it works, to human life as well, hinting that we can predict our behaviour as part of the universal trail of causation. Einstein encouraged scientists to adopt 'an objective and *causal* attitude toward the cosmos' (my italics).[63]

Speaking of Kant and internal causes, I would like to spend a few minutes on the vital role of human reason in determining the future. Kant states that the operation of reason is not subject to 'the conditions of time' and seems to be a superior power to all other inner qualities of human beings: 'it cannot be said of reason, that the state in which it determines the will is always preceded by some other state determining it... Reason is consequently the permanent condition of all actions of the will... Each action is determined in the empirical character of the man, even before it has taken place.'[64]

What Kant appears to be saying is that human behaviour is just as causal as it is in nature, subject to laws, but that the one faculty we have which is capable of rising above nature to play itself a determining role, is reason. It's a 'faculty which can spontaneously originate a series of events'.[65] This opens the way for the role of free will (and personal moral accountability[66]) in the midst of a highly deterministic universe.

Reason, in other words, as a strong source of power, is at the top of the 'food chain' of causation and enjoys an unmatched freedom to act and think. It's as if reason does not exist 'in' time and is usually at the start of a chain of events. Free-willed humans are often agents of change.

The other significant kind of internal cause arises from what we've called the teleological or purpose-driven nature of the universe. We have purpose-driven causation which is when changes come about as something evolves to fulfil its purpose: for example, when an organism grows according to its genome or when a technology is improved to better achieve its purpose. In these examples, the source of change is inside the object, recalling Aristotle's words that 'a thing's nature involves purpose'.[67] Some writers refer to exemplary causes which are ideas or models of a desired effect in the intellect and are brought into reality through action. For example, a sculptor has a design in his or her mind and actualises that design through the actions of sculpting. These internal causes are said to preconceive the effect. Aristotle called the end or purpose of an action the 'final' cause. We will stick with describing these purposes which have a causal influence as 'internal' causes.

By contrast to internal causes, external causes involve a physical impact from a material force or energy from something stronger to something weaker. That is, external causes, also known as extrinsic, originate in a material source in the external world.

The fourth aspect of a causation model, following contextualisation, definition and taxonomy, is measurement. In this section, we'll touch on the four other types of causes not yet mentioned. What is important to measure about causation, especially for the futurist? Once we've identified the source of the cause, whether internal or external, we need to investigate the respective influences of various causes. As Aristotle said, 'All change is from something to something'[68] Measurement of change will involve identifying the total conditions and causes which were sufficient to produce changes to the effect(s).

I suggest some, or all, of the following fifteen aspects could be identified and measured:

1. What caused the change(s)? → Identify main contributing force of event.

2. Was the primary cause external or internal? → Categorise as either primarily internally or externally driven event.

3. What were the secondary causes, including background causes? → Identify all secondary causes.

4. What change(s) actually took place? → Define the main change brought about.

5. What was the strength or intensity of the impacts of each cause? → Give weighting to primary and secondary causes depending on their influence.

6. What pathways did the process of change take, i.e. was there a chain of connected causes? → Construct diagram of causal structure underlying event.[69]

7. Were there any tools or instruments of causation? → Identify any instruments used for action(s) producing the effect(s).

8. What was the nature of the change(s)? → Describe what kind of change took place (movement, quality or quantity).

9. Did the change realise an ideal, idea, plan, template or mental design? → Determine any intellectual cause of the change event, such as a design, an intention, a plan.

10. What was the extent, degree or scale of the change(s)? → Decide on the magnitude of the change.

11. Over what time duration did the process of change take place? → Measure the time taken for the change event.

12. What were the stages/phases in the process of change? → Divide the change event/process into stages.

13. How permanent will the resulting change(s) be? → Assess how long the changed effect is likely to remain in place.

14. What energy was expended in the production of the effect by the cause(s)? → Describe the force/energy/momentum/power which actually brought about the change.

15. Is the same kind of change likely to happen again, and, if so, when? → Determine if similar changes are likely to happen in future and then assess the probable time frame for the recurrence of the change event.

Hume established that inferring effects from causes will proceed either from observation of an actual occurrence or through inference from similar causation in the past.[70] In addition to using valid methods of inference, the investigator should note different rules of causation which seem to work.

Since we're looking for the entities or forces that influence specific objects the most in any given cause-and-effect relation during a process of change, let's explain what an influence is. The word comes from a Latin term meaning 'flowing in' which, transliterated, means the 'capacity to have an effect on the character, development or behaviour of someone or something'.[71] Influence is the power to shape something else. That indicates a power relationship between a stronger and a weaker party. Power is simply the capacity to get something done, from the Latin word *posse*, 'the capacity or ability to direct or influence the behaviour of others or the course of events'.[72] Causation is the power of one entity or condition to shift behaviour of an object consistently and repeatedly.

Synonyms for the word 'influence' include efficacy, power, force, energy and productive capacity. Hume speaks of the cause's 'power of production'[73] and it is clear that production is probably the closest synonym to causation. He sees a cause as the production principle.[74]

Having grasped the nature of the transaction, transfer or exchange happening during causal events, a few rules to bear in mind while drawing a full picture of a causal event would be:

• Be aware of complexity and the compounding, complicating effects of many causes: 'There is no phaenomenon in nature, but what is compounded and modified by so many different circumstances...'[75] – sometimes there are joint or combined effects.

- Proximity determines causal primacy: 'Contiguous objects must have an influence much superior to the distant and remote.'[76]

- Stronger bodies tend to cause more change than weaker bodies – some bodies have more energy than others and are able to cause things to happen.

- The effect is always proportionate to the magnitude of the cause[77] so assign a weighting or relative importance to each cause – 'We are to admit no more causes of natural things than such as are both true and sufficient to explain their appearances. Therefore to the same natural effects we must, as far as possible, assign the same causes.'[78]

- Consider Aristotle's three kinds of changes – of place (movement), of quality (alteration) and of quantity (increase or decrease),[79] the most common of which is the first, movement.

The model of causation illustrated in Figure 11 has been defined and described, step by step. But what is its relevance to futurology?

The future is written in the language of causes. Future events and conditions pre-exist in their causes.

Here's how Aquinas explains that in philosophical terms: 'future things can be known in two ways, in themselves and in their causes ... we too can know things as they exist in their causes. And we know future things with scientific certitude if they exist in their causes as causes from which they necessarily result. And if future things exist in their causes in such a way that they result from the causes in most cases, then we can know them by inference more or less certain as the causes are more or less inclined to produce such effects.'[80] Note that Aquinas uses the words 'with scientific certitude'. We're aiming in this book to produce a science of future study.

The certainty here resides in the deterministic nature of causation which Kant describes as the 'time-determination by a preceding cause'.[81] There is a chain, or train, of interconnected causes leading in an observable and logical sequence into the future through continuous time. Hume envisaged this as follows: 'Here is a connected chain of natural causes and voluntary actions; but the mind feels no difference between them, in passing from one link to another; Nor is less certain of the future event than if it were connected with the objects present to the memory or senses, by a train of causes, cemented together by what we are pleased to call a physical necessity.'[82]

Read Kant's description, too: 'Every action, in so far as it is productive of an event, is itself an event or occurrence, and presupposes another preceding state, in which its cause existed. Thus that everything happens is but a continuation of a series... The actions of natural causes are, accordingly, themselves effects, and presuppose causes preceding them in time.'[83]

The idea of a train, or chain, of causation is consistent both with the continuity of time and with the continuity of the process of change. Kant says: 'the state of a thing passes in the process of a change ... to its second state...'[84] This idea is also in keeping with the principle of antecedence already discussed.

It can be said that the principles of the theory of evolution dovetail with those of time as a progression: 'Thus, as time contains the sensible condition *a priori* of the possibility of a continuous progression of that which exists to that which follows it, the understanding, by virtue of the unity of apperception, contains the condition *a priori* of the possibility of a continuous determination of the position in time of all appearances, and by this means the series of causes and effects, the former of which necessitate the sequence of the latter, and thereby render universally and for all time, and by consequence, objectively valid the empirical knowledge of the relations of time.'[85]

It's noteworthy that Hume and Kant were both confident that causation, as backed up by the necessity of laws of nature and built-in relationships in an interdependent universe, enabled knowledge of the future. Hume's words 'necessity' and 'certain' in the previous extract echo Aquinas' term I quoted: 'scientific certitude'. We're not talking about guesswork here, but about rigorous causal analysis.

The causal model, in sum, enables a full scientific investigation of the future.

Paul and Hall explain the usefulness of this approach as follows: 'According to advocates of this approach, in order to analyse the causal structure of any situation, we must first provide a "causal model" for it... Causal modelling approaches do an excellent job of representing causal dependency structures, and for this reason, are enormously influential. The main virtue of causal modelling is that it gives us a way to use known causal structure to discover or determine further causal structure and to predict the results of certain interventions on a system... Causal modelling has been proven to have enormous value, especially when it is deployed in the social sciences to represent complex causal structures or to develop sophisticated causal explanations.'[86]

Equipped with a causal model, which is logical and scientifically sound, we can become detectives of the future, building accurate pictures of the future world.

But first we need to develop the gift of foresight. And since the future must occur in four dimensions, as we'll see in the next chapter, we'll all need to develop 4D vision.

4

The future is 4D

'There is no more common-place statement than that the world in which we live is a four-dimensional space–time continuum.'

Albert Einstein, *Relativity* (1916)

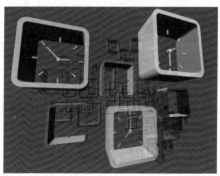

Figure 12: The 4D world of cube clocks
(© AndreasG/123RF.com)

I'm no fan of donning 3D glasses to watch movies but I do advocate 4D vision for daily life. And you don't need special glasses to see the world in four dimensions. But what precisely is the 4D world Einstein thought so commonplace?

Look at the cube clocks in Figure 12. They demonstrate Einstein's 4D world. Each cube has three directions in space – height, depth and width – plus one direction in time – forwards. With a timepiece embedded into one of the cube's faces, these four dimensions seem integrated into one continuum. The space–time continuum is like that.

And those are the four dimensions in which we live out our lives. We're all inside space, in which time is ticking.

Time and space belong together in a marriage of the four dimensions called the space–time continuum. It's been proven that time literally slows down when an object travels at very high speeds and speeds up as one moves away from a source of gravity. This reveals that time is not independent of spatial factors like speed and gravity. Rather, it's integrated into space like the clock on the cubes in Figure 12 above. It's therefore not surprising that time deeply affects the way things behave in the world. They age. They change. They work in cycles, in seasons, in defined time periods.

4D vision is the awareness that time is present with us as we journey through our world, bringing continuous change to ourselves and to our world. In addition to bringing change, time delivers the hidden order of regularity described in the previous chapter.

While we're asleep, we're still moving through time. Even a stationary object is travelling – through the time dimension. Time ticks in space. Time is ceaselessly at work in space.

Furthermore, there's a reciprocal relation between space and time as illustrated by the principle of a fixed quota of what is called space–time speed. This principle is lucidly explained by Brian Cox and Jeffrey Forshaw in their entertaining and illuminating book *Why Does E=mc² ?: (and why should we care?)*. If you use up speed in space, you have to give up some time in proportion to how much speed you use so that the exact quota of your total 'space–time speed' stays the same. Correspondingly, if you give up speed in space, you have more time to use up in your space–time speed allowance. The constancy of space–time speed shows conclusively that there is a reciprocal relation between space and time which I've described as being like a marriage.

Although I don't enjoy ageing, I'm grateful for time, without which there would be no life, evolution or change. Things would be so static and inert that they'd be dead. So time brings dynamism. It also brings regularity, from the passage of day and night and the seasons to the time periods and lifecycles in which everything operates.

Think of the world as a living 3D cube with a built-in time device ticking away inside it. That ticking timepiece you can almost hear in the universe brings both life and order. It's your friend, not your enemy.

Einstein considered 4D vision commonplace. But, then again, he was a genius. All phenomena should be measured by a time dimension – the when – as well as by the where, namely, the three coordinates of space (length, breadth and height). That's because we're never in any place except at a given time. Together, all our timed-based locations – where we were at what time – make up our life's worldline.

In order to be time-literate citizens of the future, it's imperative to cultivate 4D vision. It's the most important instrument in the intellectual toolkit of the citizen of the future.

It seems implausible to me, if not downright impossible, to think that space, and things in space, would obey laws of nature, while time, and things in time, wouldn't. That's why I've got confidence about modelling the future. Physics has proved space and time always go together in a 4D world that is living, evolving and changing.

It is crystal clear to me that all things really do behave cyclically and predictably over time. Why would one dimension of these four interconnected dimensions – time – behave radically differently from the other three? Why wouldn't all four dimensions behave according to the cosmological laws of physics, including time, including the future?

To counteract the almost universal scepticism about the future we see in our world today, we can ponder on the amazing implications of this cosmic marriage of space–time. It's a union or fusion. In this context, the future is simply what happens next in space–time. We're part of its unfolding. We continuously witness its never-ending, law-like evolution.

This book will present the case that time is just as law-like as nature itself. That's because time is enmeshed within the physical processes of life in Einstein's 4D world, like the clock in the cube.

For that reason, it's never surprising to me when I read about underlying temporal patterns of human and social behaviour which have been uncovered by sociologists, economists, demographers, game theorists, investors or historians. Many of these patterns of social behaviour observed over regular time periods will be discussed in subsequent chapters. These patterns are the living embodiments of time's work. Regularity is the heartbeat of time. Further, these patterns of behaviour provide us with templates for viewing future developments. Time obeys rules just like everything else in the universe. Without question, the future has a hidden order open to study.

In short, it appears that the dynamics of time has been seriously underestimated, even overlooked. Conquering the spatial world of Earth and outer space has been a skewed progress. Humanity took a 3D approach to a 4D world.

The 4D world was first revealed to us in all its glory by Einstein. Humanity has traversed, explored and colonised 3D space without taking into proper account the all-important fourth dimension of time. No wonder several unsustainable social and economic practices, some of which imperil the future of civilisation, have been developed.

Perhaps it's this dimensional blindness which led society to try to possess, and use, the Earth's resources without thinking about their limits or about the long-term consequences of human activity on the environment. Perhaps that's why people often engage in hyper-competition to grab power and get rich, often at the expense of others further down the food chain, without factoring in the future impacts of fracturing society by turning nation against nation, empire against empire, class against class, race against race, gender against gender and rich against poor. All of this short-termism may well have arisen from a blindfolded form of progress, employing blinkered 3D vision.

Einstein's 4D vision can save civilisation.

Citizens of the future will embrace a 4D world.

Society can only leave short-termism behind when vision is elevated to four dimensions. To date, progress has made us materially better off yet more short-sighted and more short term in our thinking, rather than less. That's largely because the great meaning of time was too often overlooked, narrowing our study of time to history. A 4D perspective includes measurement of, and sensitivity to, the time dimension, factoring in understanding of time cycles. Think back to the ticking of the cube clocks.

We humans are inside the 'cube clock' of space–time. We're deeply affected by both spatial and temporal dimensions. As Aristotle explained, 'everything in time is bound to be contained by time, just as anything which is in anything; anything in place, for instance, is bound to be contained by place ... a thing is in time, its existence will be measured by time'.[87]

Most thinkers and futurists today know that our world is likely to implode, environmentally, economically and socially, if we continue along our current path of short-term thinking. In our ignorance of the future, we make untold unwise decisions, develop abortive strategies and create malfunctioning systems.

Do we not need 4D vision to redirect us away from wrong paths?

Imagine the dynamism which would be unleashed by knowing more about how things behave over time, whether civilisations, peoples, technologies, systems or natural resources, from energy to commodities?

What we find when applying a scientific approach to the study of time, and to the future, is that everything develops through time cycles. In turn, these cycles provide patterns for accurately observing and predicting how phenomena are bound to behave in the next phases of their cycles of development.

With everything behaving in cycles through time, the world becomes open for anticipation and prediction.

There are laws of nature, including cosmic and evolutionary principles, as well as social and human laws. But are there laws of time, too?

It's pretty universally accepted that time is the medium of change.[88] The previous chapter showed that change, in turn, is caused. Aristotle stated 'the source of change is a cause'.[89] He also defined time as 'a number of continuous change' since 'things come to be and cease to be in time, increase in time, alter in time, and move in time'.[90]

This means time is an instrument of change through causation. Causal influence is both teleological and pervasive. It arises in all interactions between entities, and between entities and forces. The world, an interdependent place of multiple systems, is a cauldron of causal influences. Causes, in turn, may be studied, effects can be predicted.

We're edging towards an understanding of time's hidden order. Aristotle also stated: 'Nature is the subject of our enquiry, and nature is a principle of change, so if we do not understand the process of change, we will not understand nature either.'[91] If change is the essence of nature, as the great Greek philosopher believed, and if change is caused, as the world's major thinkers contend, and – further – if time and space are truly fused, as Einstein proved, it follows that the future of the world, produced by all the structured forces of change, should be as open to scientific enquiry as nature itself.

As time, under the influence of Einstein's physics, loses its mystery and gains, rather, a physical profile as the medium of all change,[92] it will take its rightful place at the very core of the study of the future: 'Scientific knowledge of nature involves taking magnitudes, and change and time into consideration.'[93] It's appropriate to understand and to measure time, which is 'everywhere and present alike to all things'.[94] Kant would agree, saying, 'All appearances in general, that is, all objects of the senses, are in time, and stand necessarily in relations of time.'[95]

All in all, it's possible to identify universal properties of time, or what Spengler called time's *logic*. Here are five properties to consider.

The first principle of time is that it's a process within the spatial universe.

The second property of time is that it moves in one direction only – forwards. This means two things. First, we cannot move backwards in time. No processes go in reverse order. They follow a succession of steps. In all of history no one has ever witnessed any physical actions happening backwards; there's no reverse gear for nature. The second implication of the forward direction of time is that it means nothing ever stands still or remains the same, not even the eternal-seeming mountains.

This brings us to the third principle of time: time dictates that change is life and life is change. As we go forward in time, we change: ageing, evolving, developing. The option to stay the same is removed, non-existent. Change is unchanging. Time, in short, is the channel of continuous change.

In many ways, change is binary. Everything is either in the process of improving, becoming more favourable, or declining, getting worse, all in various degrees of intensity. Everything has a built-in tendency to change for better or for worse. So time continuously creates advantages and disadvantages, that is, changes which are positive or negative. Each moment in time is a junction, either moving towards something better or something worse. Time may be a physical process as the fourth dimension of our existence but it is qualitative in its effects, producing either improvement or decline, progression or deterioration.

Both physics and philosophy have noticed that time can bring a lot of disorder with it. Aristotle said, 'In its own right, time is responsible for destruction rather than generation, because it is a number of change, and change removes present properties.'[96] Hawking's thermodynamic time arrow brought with it the challenge of entropy in *A Brief History of Time*.

For humans, however, possessed of reason, imagination and creativity, time brings qualitative change, with opportunities to build order through strategic interventions in natural and social processes. For us alone, time produces destiny, or the rational pursuit of order and balance.

The fourth principle of time is that it is continuous, occurring as a powerful, fast flow forwards rather than a series of disconnected points, linking past, present and future into one evolutionary unity. 'It is because magnitude is continuous that change is too, and because change is continuous, time is too.'[97]

What does it mean that time is continuous? A continuum is infinitely divisible, as explained by Aristotle: 'By a continuum I mean that which is divisible into parts which are always further divisible.'[98] Time, he said, is continuous: 'The now is what holds time together ... since it makes past and future time a continuous whole; and it is a limit of time, in the sense that it is the beginning of one time and the end of another ... But it does divide time potentially, and in so far as it does, it is always different; but in so far as it joins one time to another, it is always the same ... the now too is in one way a division of time, but only potentially, and in another a limit of both past and future, unifying the two. The division and the unification are the same, and they involve the same thing, but in terms of what they are, they are different.'[99]

He compares the now to a mathematical point on a line – it is different yet the line 'is the same all the way along the line'.[100] In the same way, the now – or present – is the end of past time and the beginning of future time, connecting all phases of time into a whole, with each moment like a point on a long line.

This means that change will tend to be cumulative over time, building on past evolution in longer-term developmental processes.

There are, therefore, deep interconnections between past, present and future. This fact about time mitigates the effects of change, pointing to the reality that most change will always be evolutionary rather than revolutionary.

The fifth and final basic property of time is that it's finite, even though it operates on an enormous cosmological scale (see Appendix 1: Timelines of time). It's long term, or deep, with the universe about 13.7 billion years old. Perhaps we cannot even truly conceive of that span of time. Nevertheless, it shows the universe of space–time had a definite beginning. Cosmologists have also looked deep in the future of the universe and the end of its incredible, unimaginable lifespan.

Some cycles in the world operate over millions of years, some over thousands of years, still others over centuries or decades. As a civilisation, we need to respect and revere deep time. We need a balanced time perspective as part of our 4D vision of the world.

Time, then, is both very deep and yet finite. That everything is finite in space–time creates the concept of the lifespan as well as the lifecycle. The latter is the span of development between beginning or birth, and the end or death. Since there is continuity of time, in addition to continuous change, there will naturally be evolutionary change on a monumental scale. Lifecycles throughout the cosmos effectively mean things behave in cyclical ways throughout their lifespans. This fact, arising from a key principle of time, is vital to the practice of futurology since it enables prefigurement, or preconstruction, of the future through plotting development on a lifecycle trajectory. This technique will be extensively explained and illustrated in Chapter 7.

The finite nature of existence in space–time means there are limits which set boundaries for possibilities. Organisms have a lifecycle of birth, development, decline and death. Nothing lasts forever. Soon or later, every entity and every system will come up against its limits, whether its mortality, its disadvantages compared to competitors, its declining powers or the temporary or permanent scarcity of resources. The way systems grow and meet their natural limits is one reason why they operate in cycles.

The five principles in Figure 13 highlight the lawful nature of time within space–time. The extent to which a phenomenon may be known indicates whether it can be predicted. This book will illustrate how things behave in, or across, time. The lawful nature of time points to the lawfulness of the future.

The objective of futurology is to track the expected behaviour of entities and systems in the future phase of time using 4D logic. This includes an understanding of how time works. As historians, economists and sociologists track regularities they see in history and development, so futurists may track regularities of cyclical behaviour across the continuity of time far into the 4D future.

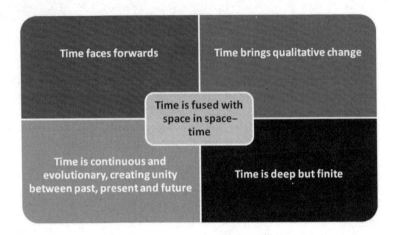

Figure 13: Five principles of time

But even when we're armed with 4D vision and look at how things work in their evolving space–time world, is there enough understanding of how reality works to produce a complete science of foreknowledge, a science of the future so robust that it would have been approved by the great minds of modern science and philosophy, including Bacon, Descartes, Newton, Hume, Kant, Hegel, Einstein and Hawking?

5
The rise of scientific foresight

'The universe is governed by two kinds of laws, laws of evolution, which determine how the universe develops in time, given its state at one time, and boundary conditions which determine the initial state.'

Stephen Hawking,
Stephen Hawking and the Theory of Everything
(Channel 4 and Discovery TV documentary, 2008)

Foresight will be scientific when it is based on laws of nature, the universal law of causation and on an understanding of time's role as the medium of change.

Hegel set himself the task of raising philosophy 'to the status of a Science', believing that truth takes shape within the discipline of science: 'knowing should be Science', he said.[101] The reason science and philosophy have been converging over the centuries is that they are both searching for factual truth. This book is about uncovering the order behind the future so it can be studied systematically.

In the preface to the first edition of his masterpiece *Critique of Pure Reason*, Kant set the bar high for knowledge: 'For it is a necessary condition of all knowledge that is to be established upon *a priori* grounds, that it shall be held to be absolutely necessary.'[102] The *a priori* knowledge Kant is talking about has to be true independently of subjective experience. It must carry the logical quality of necessity. Kant indicated that only reason, not the senses, could acquire this kind of pure knowledge: 'For reason is the faculty which furnishes us with the principles of knowledge *a priori*.'[103]

George Boole, the English mathematician, philosopher and pioneer of modern logic, pointed out the goal of science in these words: 'The object of science ... is the knowledge of laws and relations. To be able to distinguish what is essential to this end, from what is only accidentally associated with it, is one of the most important conditions of scientific progress.'[104]

The science, in other words, is in the laws. Such laws are 'rules of necessary existence'.[105] The aim in this work is to prove there's science in the future, too, that it is fashioned and formed according to universal laws.

Table 1 below encapsulates six principles for producing foreknowledge using scientific thinking based on this kind of 'knowledge of laws and relations'.

First principle – The laws and formulas of nature establish sufficient regularity in the world to enable modelling.

Hawking explains the importance of regularity to science: 'Today most scientists would say a law of nature is a rule that is based upon an observed regularity and provides predictions that go beyond the immediate situations upon which it is based.'[107]

Let's exemplify this point by looking again at the periodic table. It's the foundation of modern chemistry because it contains all the known elements composing the world's solids, gases, liquids and synthetics. It outlines, in order, repeated patterns of characteristics in the elements making up the material world (118 elements, and counting, of which about 90 occur naturally). The knowledge contained in the periodic table enables us to explain how material things behave and react.

Principle	Examples	Relevance for foreknowledge
The laws and formulas of nature establish sufficient regularity in the world to enable modelling.	Newton's laws of motion and universal gravitation;[106] mutual gravitation holds celestial bodies in position; Force = inertial mass x acceleration (Newton); Einstein's absolute speed of light and formula $E=mc^2$; the laws of thermodynamics, the Standard Model of Particle Physics; laws of evolutionary development; the periodic table; Euler's theorem, etc.	Under the surface of continuous change are permanencies and regularities, often reflected in the laws of nature; Conformity to the built-in principles of existence produces much regular, understood and predictable behaviour.

Human behaviour is universal.	Human needs, wants, desires and aspirations have been constant throughout history; game theory assumes individuals nearly always act out of strategic self-interest; cause and effect relations link human psychology and actions.	We exhibit predictable self-interested behaviour within the bounds of nature, psychology and society.
Change and development occur through cyclical processes.	Cycles of recurrent behaviour have been observed in cosmology, biology, history, economics, business, politics and sociology.	Cycles are patterns in long-term behaviour and futurists can use past evolution and present position to project future trajectories along these cycles.

All causes have consequent outcomes.	All change is caused. The world is highly causal. Each action produces a reaction. A decision to carry out an action can cause the action itself.	Effects occur in the future and may be predicted, from their causes, based on past behaviour. Effects pre-exist in their causes.
Every entity and organism in the universe is a machine-like system interacting with other systems.	From the Milky Way and the solar system to our human bodies, from households to organisations, from communities to civilisations, everything functions as a system. Everything's purpose functions as a cause of actions as it strives to fulfil its inherent purpose.	Systems have universal characteristics and in that sense their behaviour occurs within a framework in which it can be understood and anticipated.

Nothing happens in a vacuum.	In physics, antecedence is a view that everything emerges from a pre-existing state and spends its time interacting with its life-giving evolving environment.	There are observable patterns of interaction and mutual influence. Random occurrences are the exception rather than the norm. What is not random is predictable.

Table 1: Six principles of scientific foresight

The order in which each element is arranged depends on its specific atomic structure, with a unique number of protons in its nucleus as well as electrons moving around the nucleus. The table begins with the lightest element which has the simplest atom structure, namely hydrogen. Hydrogen has the atomic number of 1 because it has only one proton orbited by one electron.

By arranging the elements in this order, predictions can be made at a glance about an element's properties, such as whether it will be reactive or inert and what other elements it will interact with. The periodic table's inventor, Mendeleev, originally used it to predict the properties of as yet undiscovered elements, correctly anticipating, for example, the properties of gallium and germanium.[108]

It's not just the elements, or even the planets, which behave with sufficient regularity to enable modelling. Energy and matter interact according to the famous universal formula discovered by Einstein, namely $E=mc^2$. Time itself is locked into space and everything in it has a lifespan made up of lifecycles, or distinct periods. And major philosophers, ancient, medieval and modern, have agreed that all changes are caused, with the world being therefore highly causal. In the light of these laws and formulas, I don't see how anyone can seriously doubt the inherent lawfulness of the universe.

Second principle – Human behaviour is universal.

I no longer believe that human behaviour is unpredictable. Philosopher David Hume put it this way: 'A man who at noon leaves his purse full of gold on the pavement at Charing-Cross may as well expect that it will fly away like a feather, as that he will find it untouched an hour after. Above one half of human reasonings contain inferences of a similar nature, attended with more or less degrees of certainty, proportioned to our experience of the usual conduct of mankind in such particular situations.'[109]

Hume included human nature within the cause and effect structures of the world. That is, he regarded human behaviour as causal: 'Thus it appears, not only that the conjunction between motives and voluntary actions is as regular and uniform, as that between the cause and effect in any part of nature; but also that this regular conjunction has been universally acknowledged among mankind, and has never been the subject of dispute, either in philosophy or common life.'[110]

For Hume, then, causation is at work within human nature, as it is in nature as a whole. In fact, he goes as far as to claim that causation is crucial to personal identity: 'memory does not so much produce as discover personal identity, by shewing us the relation of cause and effect among our different perceptions'.[111] Without cause and effect connections between ideas, impressions, memories and experiences, how would a person's identity hold together? For these reasons, Hume explains how central causation is to human consciousness: 'the same person may vary his character and disposition, as well as his impressions and ideas, without losing his identity. Whatever changes he endures, his several parts are still connected by the relation of causation... Had we no memory, we never shou'd have any notion of causation, nor consequently of that chain of causes and effects, which constitute our self or person.'[112]

At base, human nature operates by a common mechanism: 'It is universally acknowledged, that there is a great uniformity among the actions of men, in all nations and ages, and that human nature remains still the same, in its principles and operations. The same motives always produce the same actions. The same events follow from the same causes... Mankind are so much the same, in all times and places, that history informs us of nothing new or strange in this particular. Its chief use is only to discover the constant and universal principles of human nature, by shewing men in all varieties of circumstances and situations, and furnishing us with materials, from which we form our observations, and become acquainted with the regular springs of human action and behaviour.'[113]

Two of these regular springs of action are pain and pleasure: 'The pain and pleasure, therefore, being the primary causes of vice and virtue, must also be the causes of all their effects, and consequently of pride and humility...'[114]

The same uniformity of behaviour can be observed at the level of society: 'How could politics be a science, if laws and forms of government had not a uniform influence upon society? Where would be the foundation of morals, if particular characters had no certain or determinate power to produce particular sentiments, and if these sentiments had no constant operation on actions?'[115]

Game theory has successfully used this apparent uniformity of human nature to predict decision making, arguing that individuals nearly always act strategically in a social context to further their self-interest. And could we even have a science of psychology if there was no underlying uniformity to human behaviour? It's difficult to see how human nature can be isolated from the cause and effect structure of the world. In fact, that's just not possible.

Third principle – Change and development occur through cyclical processes.

It was established in Chapter 3 that all change is caused, as illustrated in Figure 10. There's an underlying structure to change.

It's clear from the comprehensive role of evolution in nature and society that organisms and things develop in structured processes over identifiable time spans. In Chapter 7, these time spans and cycles of development will be explained in detail. A variety of demographers, economists, sociologists, political philosophers and historians have identified periodic and repeated cycles of development in their respective fields.

For the futurologist, these cycles provide a template (time-pattern) for making predictions about future evolution.

Fouth principle – All causes have consequent outcomes.

The doctrine of causation outlined in Chapter 3 showed causation to be the universal principle of scientific knowledge of our world. Aquinas argued centuries ago that effects pre-exist in their causes. We may use causation to gain foreknowledge of how its effects will be distributed.

As already stated, the world is highly causal. This means its future can be modelled. Things are not as unpredictable as many thinkers have suggested.

There is also a built-in accountability that comes with this model for understanding potential outcomes of actions, decisions, plans and policies and being proactive in preventing negative outcomes and promoting positive ones.

Fifth principle – Every entity and organism in the universe is a machine-like system interacting with other systems.

What isn't a system? There's the solar system. There's Mother Earth and all her ecosystems. There's the system of the human body, along with all its sub-systems.[116] There are the systems families develop to operate their daily households. There's the atomic system of the nucleus and the orbiting electrons making up the elements of matter. There are systems and sub-systems of organisations and societies. And so it goes on.

Systems thinking shows how systems behave in universal ways and interact with other systems.

It seems automation of natural processes of growth, evolution and development is widespread throughout nature, from the zygote which contains the genome of a human individual, to the evolutionary instincts of creatures.

There's a machine-like efficiency to nature and to systems which provides a foundation for managing and engineering social order. Machines, and automatic processes, are, by and large, predictable once their mechanisms are known.

Sixth principle – Nothing happens in a vacuum.

David Bohm's principle of antecedence, whereby everything emerges from something else, from a pre-existing state or conditions, is consistent with the causal nature of the world in which all changes are caused by something else. In Chapter 3, the idea of trains or chains of causation was explored.

Both antecedence and causation have in common the concept of interdependence, by which no organism, or thing, is an island. Rather, entities are dependent on other entities and systems, interacting with them in what Biomatrix theory describes as a web of interconnecting systems.

If causation is happening everywhere all of the time, and if antecedence is true, what can really happen in a vacuum?

What this means for futurology is that foreknowledge needs to be highly contextualised, since the future emerges holistically through a combination of multiple factors. The key, as we have seen, is to read the causes, both underlying conditions as well as primary causes, of the future.

In summary, the six principles for producing scientific foresight are:

- The regularity of the world enables modelling.

- Human behaviour is universal.

- Change and development happen through cycles.

- All causes have consequent outcomes.

- Everything is a system.

- Nothing happens in a vacuum.

Taking into account these principles will improve understanding of the structure of changes ushering in the future. Together, they form the foundation for a science of the future.

In addition, scientific foreknowledge would also need to satisfy the principles of logic, to which we now turn.

6

A logic of the future

'What the vulgar call chance is nothing but a secret and concealed cause.'

David Hume,
A Treatise of Human Nature (1739–40)

In my first book, *Knowing our Future – the startling case for futurology*, I argued that futurology should hold itself accountable to a narrow band of truth ranging from certain knowledge, based on direct causational influences, to highly probable knowledge. This can be visualised.

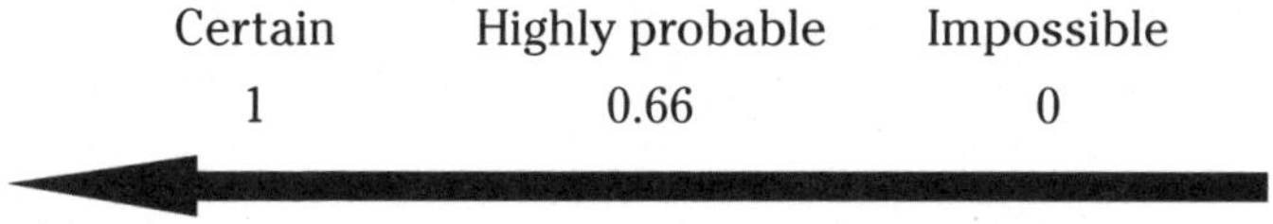

Certain	Highly probable	Impossible
1	0.66	0

Figure 14: Narrow band of truth (←) for futurology on probability scale

On this scale, probability is usually measured on a scale of 0 to 1, with 0 denoting impossibility and 1 indicating certainty or something which is bound to happen: 'The probability of a proposition that is certainly true, or an event that is sure to happen, is 1.'[117]

The causal model in Figure 11 provided a framework for developing prognostic insight, or foresight. Through identification of real causes of the future, it's possible to stay within the narrow band of truth.

It's interesting that probability, according to Keynes, is only 'a lower degree of rational belief than certainty'.[118] It's important to see the logic behind probability – its degree of rationality. There's nothing shameful about probable knowledge. In a series of lectures in 1795, Laplace posited that our entire system of knowledge hinged largely on probabilities. He defined probability as a fraction we can measure 'whose numerator is the number of favourable cases and whose denominator is the number of all the cases possible'.[119] Put in another way, probability is calculated as 'the ratio of the number of favourable cases to that of all the cases possible'.[120] A good example of probable knowledge would be the mortality tables of actuaries, which Laplace calls a table of the probability of human life. The probability becomes 'the sum of the possibilities of each favourable case'.[121] When all the cases are favourable to an event, he went on, the probability changes to certainty.

Part of the logic of the future is the calculation of probability in terms of how close to certainty we can get in our predictions. Using his mathematics of probability, Laplace worked out a theory for predicting the likelihood of future events. What he called his seventh principle states: 'The probability of a future event is the sum of the products of the probability of each cause, drawn from the event observed, by the probability that, this cause existing, the future event will occur.'[122] He was proposing to use causes to determine the likelihood of any given event happening in the future.

Laplace saw there was sufficient regularity in the world to allow for logical and valid predictions: 'All events, even those which on account of their insignificance do not seem to follow the great laws of nature, are a result of it just as necessarily as the revolutions of the sun.'[123] Events are always tied to what he described as the entire system of the universe.

Hume, despite being a sceptic, went as far as to deny the reality of chance, so ingrained did he believe causation was in the world: 'It is universally allowed, that nothing exists without a cause of its existence, and that chance, when strictly examined, is a mere negative word, and means not any real power, which has anywhere, a being in nature.'[124]

Chance, he announced, has no existence.

When behaviour in nature and society obeys scientific laws, or established principles, it opens the way for predictions of their future states and outcomes. The more regular behaviour is, the more predictable it should prove to be. The Latin word *praedicere* means to 'make known beforehand' and predictions make statements about what is going to happen, often as a consequence of certain causes, both direct and indirect.

It will be useful at this point to examine the concept of regularity in more detail. Regularity is defined by the *New Oxford Dictionary of English* as 'arranged in, or constituting, a constant or definite pattern ... recurring at short uniform intervals ... arranged in, or constituting, a symmetrical or harmonious pattern ... conforming to ... an accepted standard of procedure or convention'.[125] Synonyms for regularity derived from this definition would be words like: pattern, arrangement, symmetry and even template; that is, something which has a definite form, like a stencil, which can be replicated. The pattern has to be persistent, due to fixed relationships.

Laplace was convinced that scientific knowledge had advanced sufficiently to allow for valid foresight: 'discoveries in mechanics and geometry, added to that of universal gravity, have enabled [the human mind] to comprehend in the same analytical expressions the past and future states of the system of the world. Applying the same method to some other objects of its knowledge, it has succeeded in referring to general laws observed phenomena and in foreseeing those which given circumstances ought to produce.'[126]

Think of how useful Laplace's method of calculating probabilities can be to individuals, organisations and societies. Probability can measure for us the likelihood of a result, an outcome or a future event. We can use probability for calculating the most beneficial course of action. Even individuals could use calculations of this kind to create a more mathematically based hope: 'The word *hope*...

expresses generally the advantage of that one who expects a certain benefit in suppositions which are only probable. This advantage in the theory of chance is a product of the sum hoped for by the probability of obtaining it... We call this advantage *mathematical hope*.'[127]

Laplace's calculus for human decision making is, as we've seen, founded on mathematical probability. He thought we could weigh up favourable outcomes and unfavourable ones, looking at benefits or losses future events, or states, could bring about. Is the likely potential gain greater than the likely potential loss? The answer becomes a guide to decisions as long as it is objectively calculated: 'But it is necessary, in order to attain this, to appreciate exactly the advantages, the losses, and their respective probabilities.'[128]

By contrast, we make bad decisions if we cling to illusions and exaggerate subjective probabilities: 'The mind has its illusions as the sense of sight; and in the same manner that the sense of feeling corrects the latter, reflection and calculation correct the former. Probability based upon daily experience, or exaggerated by fear and by hope, strikes us more than a superior probability but it is only a simple result of calculus... Our passions, our prejudices, and dominating opinions, by exaggerating the probabilities which are favourable to them and by attenuating the contrary probabilities, are the abundant sources of dangerous illusions.'[129]

Needless to say, scientific foresight will be based on objective probabilities with minimal or zero interference from personal and ideological preferences. In the post-Copernican world, science places us in non-special light and it is when we unjustly place ourselves at the centre of the universe that we become subject to delusional thinking.

In our logic for the future, we're looking for rational truth about the future based on probable, and, at times, certain knowledge: 'First, there are some scientific propositions about which human speculation and reason cannot arrive at a securely demonstrated knowledge, but can only supply a probable opinion and a reasonable conjecture... There are other propositions of which we have, or can confidently expect to have, certain knowledge, by means of experiment, prolonged observation, and necessary demonstrations...'[130]

The timeless classics of science, from Aristotle's *Physics* to Einstein's *Relativity*, try to prove how the world really works. They express their findings in universal terms which satisfy the rules of reason. Science, that is, provides factual, observed evidence for its statements about the world.

Then logic, whether mathematical or philosophical, outlines how these collected facts may be turned into general truths which humanity can use. That way, we gradually build a body of trusted knowledge which we can apply to develop new technologies, wealth and social systems. This whole knowledge-based process drives civilisation forward.

Given the narrow band of truth in Figure 14, we should discuss certainty in addition to probability. Certain knowledge may be defined as clear, comprehensive, convincing and confirmed:

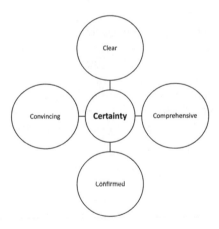

Figure 15: Criteria for certain knowledge

Knowledge is clear if it has been logically defined using scientifically understandable terms. It is comprehensive if it makes sense according to a body of existing knowledge about the world. It is convincing if counterarguments consistently fail to undermine the truth claims made about it. And it is confirmed if substantial evidence supports it.

Certain knowledge of this kind will stand the test of time. Laplace explains the process science employs to produce certainty: 'The surest method which can guide us in the search for truth, consists in rising by induction from phenomena to laws and from laws to forces. Laws are the ratios which connect particular phenomena together: when they have shown the general principle of the forces from which they are derived, one verifies it either by direct experiences ... or by examination if it agrees with known phenomena; and if by a rigorous analysis we see them proceed from this principle, even in their small details, and if, moreover, they are quite varied and very numerous, then science acquires the highest degree of certainty and of perfection that it is able to attain.'[131] Examples of certain knowledge include laws like universal gravitation and motion, facts, mathematical truths and formula.[132]

The law of causation seems to be another example of certain knowledge.

Prediction, based on foreknowledge, is an integral part of scientific philosophy: 'Scientific philosophy ... regards knowledge as an instrument of prediction and for which sense observation is the only admissible criterion of ... truth.'[133] Reichenbach claimed his ultimate goal was the 'foretelling of the rolling of the dice of the cosmos'[134] so as to control and shape the future.[135] The methods of science are tailor-made for futurists.

It's important to state that most predictive scientific knowledge is probable rather than absolutely certain: 'the theory of probability supplies the instrument of predictive knowledge as well as the form of the laws of nature; its subject is the very nerve of scientific method'.[136]

Predictive knowledge is largely probable knowledge, but the question is: how probable? According to Reichenbach, probability is based on 'frequency interpretation' and is 'the limit of a frequency': 'Probability statements express relative frequencies of repeated events, that is, frequencies counted as a percentage of the total. They are derived from frequencies observed in the past and include the assumption that the same frequencies will hold approximately for the future.

They are constructed by means of the inductive inference. If we regard the probability of heads for the tossing of a coin as being given by one-half, we mean that in repeated throws of the coin heads will turn up in 50 percent of the cases.'[137] We are all familiar with fifty-fifty situations and understand what it means when we're told there's a 75 per cent chance of something happening. Probabilities are determined by aggregating repeated events and estimating the likelihood of their recurrence. The more regular the behaviour being studied, the closer we can push probability towards certainty (which, by definition, is a hundred per cent probability).

Armed with the theory of probability and a scientific method of induction, the futurologist becomes a time detective, piecing together the puzzle of tomorrow's world, patiently building a logical hypothesis that fits all the facts.[138]

Just as a puzzle enthusiast uses a picture to help him piece together its visual patterns, so the futurologist can look at regular behaviour of his subject matter in cycles and lifespans, which are like time templates – that is, pictures of behaviour in time. They help us to foresee the future, whether we want to know the time of high tide at a local beach, make an economic forecast, anticipate expected demand for a new product or look ahead at population trends.

It is to time patterns, showing how things tend to act during definite periods, that we now turn since they are a critical part of the order of the future.

7

Cycles of time

'When we turn our attention from social disintegration to social growth, we shall recollect our finding ... that growth, like disintegration, exhibits a cyclically rhythmic movement. Growth takes place whenever a challenge evokes a successful response that, in turn, evokes a further and different challenge. We have not found any intrinsic reason why this process should not repeat itself indefinitely...'

Arnold Joseph Toynbee,
A Study of History (1934–61)

We see cycles in the four seasons, in gravitational orbits of the solar system, in ocean tides and currents, in long-range shifts of climate, in the growth of populations, in the ages of a person's life, in menstrual cycles, in the lifecycles of buildings, in the boom and bust of economies, in the annual fluctuations of consumer retail spending, in product lifecycles, in clothing fashions that come and go, in election periods and terms of office in politics and even in the rise and fall of empires and powers in history. Cycles are everywhere.

But what precisely are all these cycles of time? And how important are they for understanding the future? What role does time itself play in producing cycles of behaviour?

With such an omnipresence of cycles, it seems we live in a pendulum-like world with a high degree of predictability. Life is regularity in motion, from our heartbeats to our daily routines. The cycles we are studying in this chapter display the regular behaviour of entities. It seems that time does provide order, putting things into sequence. It unfolds built-in codes of life like DNA. It enables things to move towards their natural purposes. It creates rhythms of behaviour over recurring periods.

Before discussing time cycles, let's examine in more detail the concept of regularity. A cycle, after all, reflects regular behaviour.

In 1687, Sir Isaac Newton wrote in *Principia Mathematica*, recognised as one of science's greatest works, 'The centre of the system of the world is immovable.'

By definition, a regularity needs to be periodic. That is, it'll occur at certain time intervals. It will have a typical duration. We look for regularity in what happens but we also look for regularity in the time taken for something to happen. It could be the ocean tides, the water cycle, an economic or production cycle, a stock market cycle, a historical movement or a demographic trend. For the futurist, what's recurrent, or highly regular, in this manner, can be the basis of a prediction.

Science has always focused on understanding regularities. It's customary to formulate laws, principles, theories and models which explain the processes and mechanisms of recurrent phenomena. Once these regularities have been proven by evidence beyond a reasonable doubt, they become universal characteristics of the world we know and understand. Such knowledge can then be used throughout the world, by people of different cultures and beliefs, to solve common problems through science.

Let's go on a quick guided tour of nature and society to observe regularities and time patterns at work.

To start with, there's a highly regular motion throughout the stable solar system which is our cosmic neighbourhood. Think of the near perfect sphere shape of planets and stars. Orbits in the solar system are close to perfect circles.[139] Planets have very regular orbits 'within a few percent of circles'.[140] Thankfully, our neighbour the moon and our Earth are synchronised in their movements: 'The moon turns once as it orbits Earth: both its spin and its orbit follow cycles that repeat themselves regularly.'[141]

As is well known, our own planet completes one rotation on its axis every twenty-four hours to make each day. At the same time, it revolves around the sun in about 365.25 days to produce each year. Pretty regular stuff. We don't have 26-hour days or years of 400 days. And when one tosses a stone into a dam the ripples are neatly circular, not haphazard. Organised patterns are evident everywhere.

It's natural for humans to see beauty in such symmetry and regularity. In mathematics, for example, there's an abstract beauty and conceptual perfection. In 1751, mathematical genius Leonhard Euler (1707–83), proved that for 3D polyhedra, their vertices (V), edges (E) and faces (F) always have the relationship expressed in his formula $V-E+F = 2$. [142] This is a highly regarded and elegant theorem which expresses an abstract order and perfection in these 3D shapes. Euler also proved that there can only ever be five regular solids, given the truth of his formula and the limits it imposes on permutations for polyhedra. Regular polyhedra do occur in nature, too (for example, in some crystals). Euler's theorem expresses a universal relationship. It expresses mathematical order. It embodies a perfect regularity.

Mathematical regularities may seem more abstract than regularities observed in nature but we often design useful and ornamental products based on the inspirational order and knowledge of mathematics. The popular golf ball, for example, is typically designed with 220 hexagons and 12 pentagons for its perfectly calibrated balance.

Coming down to life at the micro scale, Kepler identified the hexagonal symmetry of snowflakes early in the seventeenth century and contemporary scientist and mathematician

Stephen Wolfram believes their formation follows a few simple rules resulting in subtle variations on a six-pointed shape. Wolfram also shows that spiral patterns in plants converge to within a degree or less of 137.5°. That's a pretty exact pattern, a widespread regularity. Wolfram has noted that the complex variety of shapes of trees and leaves is driven by one simple underlying branching pattern. Likewise, Leonardo da Vinci recognised regular patterns in how leaves are arranged on a plant stem (phyllotaxis). Mathematicians and artists seem attuned to these invisible patterns of life.

There are, then, elegant regularities in the physics of the solar system and on Earth. Tides can be accurately timetabled because they occur periodically as a result of the consistent gravity exerted by the moon on Earth's oceans as these two bodies rotate in a choreographed dance of their orbits. In 12 hours, Earth rotates 180 degrees, while the moon turns 6 degrees around the Earth in the same period of time. As a consequence, high tide will occur approximately every 12 hours and 25 minutes. This is the clockwork cosmos Newton observed. The solar system is stable and predictable.

Even the humble dung beetle navigates its direction by the stars and moon. Recent field experiments on a South African game reserve demonstrated that these cosmically sensitive insects can roll their dung balls along straight paths under starlit skies, but not when it's overcast.[143] The beetle can detect regularities in the position of stars and orientate itself by their patterns.

For Strogatz, there are regularities throughout nature in the beat of oscillators of different kinds which are highly synchronised: 'the tendency to synchronize is one of the most pervasive drives in the universe, extending from atoms to animals, from people to planets'.[144] The human heart, for example, has its own oscillator – roughly 10,000 cells responsible for generating the electric rhythm behind a typical lifetime of three billion heartbeats.[145] The brain, too, has oscillators which are responsible for the so-called circadian rhythm or 24-hour biological clock which is 'the internal chronometer that keeps us in sync with the world around us'.[146] Even though the brain is reputed to be the most complex phenomenon ever discovered, with about 100 billion neurons, operating electrically, each with an average of thousands of synapses connected to other cells, it's organised into definite areas having specific functions, all working together in one effective system.[147]

On a human social level, there is even the well-observed phenomenon of menstrual synchrony among women living together which shows yet again how regular cycles in nature can influence one another through some sort of integrating chemical exchange. These synchronisations happen beyond the conscious level and work automatically. They're built into cycles of life.

Driving these recurrences of oscillators, or clock-like cycles in nature, is the mathematics of self-organisation, the 'spontaneous emergence of order out of chaos'.[148]

Strogatz's universal oscillators unveil an essentially mechanical world pulsing behind the richly diverse and beautiful surfaces of nature.

Although the universe itself is not a Newtonian clock, but a dynamic Einsteinium space–time, it's nevertheless filled with clocks: biological clocks (oscillators in the brain and heart), including the circadian clock, planetary clocks, atomic clocks and a multitude of inanimate clocks. Their purpose is to create order, to give the universe a regular rhythm, a gigantic, automatic pulse.

In the universe and on Earth randomness is decisively trumped by regularity. Chance, as the great philosophers and scientists have argued, is just causation in disguise. Chance, far from ruling the world, plays second fiddle to the law of causation. Hume, for example, did not believe in the reality of chance. Chance, he asserted is 'universally allowed to have no existence', quipping that 'what the vulgar call chance is nothing but a secret and concealed cause.'[149]

The overriding impression created by a serious observation of both nature and society is of a celestial order in the heavens and widespread spontaneous order on Earth. In both domains, there's a superabundance of clock-like regularities.

Laplace, pioneer in the mathematics of probability, would have agreed: 'Amid the variable and unknown causes which we comprehend under the name of chance, and which render uncertain and irregular the march of events, we see appearing, in the measure that they multiply, a striking regularity which seems to hold to a design and which has been considered as proof of Providence.'[150] In the long run, the influence of causation is uncovered even in apparently irregular phenomena: 'in a series of events indefinitely prolonged the action of regular and constant causes ought to prevail in the long run over that of irregular causes'.[151]

Both the natural and social sciences, including study of the future, can exploit knowledge of regularities to build theoretical and computer models which have predictive power. This should lead to an increasing, and even escalating, use of prediction as a proactive tool for problem solving in diverse fields such as public health, criminology, retail, finance, agriculture and energy.

As Aristotle wrote in his masterpiece of scientific thought, *Physics*, we need to understand the process of change, which is from a current state to a future state, to truly understand nature.[152]

Having looked at underlying regularities, let's examine in more detail the behaviour of cycles.

I see cycles as time patterns – that is, they exhibit regularity in the dimension of time. A cycle may be defined as a series of events that is repeated in the same order on a regular, or periodic, basis.[153] Perhaps the most important kind of cycle is a lifecycle. It's a complete series or succession of stages through which an organism passes from formation to eventual death.[154] It traces the path of how unique things begin, change, grow, peak, decline and die through time, following a predictable sequence of phases. Futurists look for these measurable cycles to help them anticipate trends and developments.

In essence, then, a cycle is a succession of events or states, following a typical order, which usually occurs in a regular time period.[155]

Although the code of the future is composed of specific causes, as Chapter 3 explained, it's these broad cycles of existence which provide the outlines of the macro-future. Put another way, while cycles provide the temporal framework of the future, causes generate the momentum that actually produces it. You could say the cycles of time we're studying in this chapter constitute the context for a broad understanding of the future. The details of the picture of the future will be provided, of course, by analysis of causal influences.

Cycles of different kinds have been observed from ancient times. The Mayans developed an elaborate system of calendars spanning huge tracts of time which were used to make long-term prophecies. Aristotle pointed out that things which are living, being generated or destroyed, operate in cycles: 'This is due to the fact that ... their beginnings and endings seem to conform to a cycle. In fact, people think of time itself as a kind of cycle, and this, in turn, is because time measures that kind of movement and is itself measured by that kind of movement. And so to say that things which are generated form a cycle is to say that time is a kind of cycle, which is due to the fact that it is measured by a circular movement.'[156]

I can't think of a single entity in nature or society which isn't subject to some lifecycle, to some temporal framework in which it operates. Nor is anything isolated from cycles which are happening all over nature. These cycles, or repeatable time patterns, enable some measure of prediction about future states as entities move through, and change with, time.

Since *everything* exists in Einstein's space–time continuum, *everything* must be deeply influenced by both space and time. The laws of nature are universal and often describe how systems behave in space–time. For example, we looked at five principles of time in Chapter 4.

Biophysicist Arthur T. Winfree, a leading expert in circadian rhythms, urges us to think of Earth as a giant clock with living organisms marking time in cycles of twenty-four hours of alternating light and darkness, with human consciousness, too, ebbing and flowing in this daily cycle.[157] Winfree believes this regularised marking of time according to the basic pattern of the Earth clock is absolutely built into living things.[158]

The very survival of cultures and civilisations has always depended on mastering cycles of nature. There's considerable evidence from theoreticians in sociology, economics and history of recurring cycles and underlying patterns observed over very long periods of human time. Within specific social sciences historic regularities have been observed.

Arnold Toynbee's monumental *A Study of History*, for example, shows that there are laws of civilisation, revealed through disciplines like economics, political science and sociology.[159] In a historical study of twenty-one societies, of which five are still current, Toynbee pinpointed the universal principles behind the evolution of civilisations.

Deep down, the key feature, not just in history, but in the evolution of life, has been making the transition from a static to a dynamic state: 'This alternating rhythm of static and dynamic, of movement and pause and movement, has been regarded by many observers in many different ages as something fundamental in the nature of the Universe.'[160] Like nature, Toynbee argued, society is in 'dynamic motion along a course of change and growth'.[161]

Studying the origins of twenty-one civilisations, the historian identified the relation between humans and the environment as the key to understanding the quest for civilisation which is spurred by a serious challenge from nature which requires a collective human response to overcome: 'On the plateau the fathers of the Andean Civilization were challenged by a bleak climate and a grudging soil; on the coast they were challenged by the heat and drought of an almost rainless equatorial desert at sea-level, which could only be made to blossom as the rose by the works of man.'[162] In similar vein, Hellenic civilisation, for Toynbee, developed and expanded in response to the challenge[163] of invasions from the sea, while the Mayans fought against the harshness of the tropical forest in order to cultivate and conquer their land. In Toynbee's model of history it's the challenge from the environment which provides the stimulus provoking continued social development.

Toynbee sees the momentum driving forward a civilisation as being generated from an exceptional virtuous circle of a successful response to a challenge leading to increased vitality reinforcing ongoing responses to further challenges: 'And to convert the movement into a repetitive, recurrent rhythm, there must be an *élan vital* ... which carries the challenged party through equilibrium into an overbalance which exposes him to a fresh challenge and thereby inspires him to make a fresh response in the form of a further equilibrium ending a further overbalance, and so on in a progression that is potentially infinite.'[164]

Toynbee referred to this universal process as the 'rhythm of growth'.[165] A successful response by a society to a challenge from its environment energises its people, which, in turn, creates the capacity and will to rise to the next challenge, and so on, building momentum for growth, which further strengthens the vitality needed to take on more collective projects for the good of the society. He speaks of a formula and an elemental rhythm of challenge and response, in which success breeds success: 'In a growing civilisation a challenge meets with a successful response which proceeds to generate another and a different challenge which meets with another successful response.'[166]

Growth is both internal and external, characterised by material and technical progress and increasing cultural self-articulation of the society. Progress itself is governed by the 'law of progressive simplification' which is an 'enhancement of practical efficiency'.[167] It is true that evolution tends towards increased efficiency and this is especially true in the highly competitive arena of technology and business. Inwardly, there is a drive for a thriving society to express and determine itself; for example, Toynbee sees the West as driven towards the twin aspirations of 'Industrialism and Democracy' as defining social ideals.[168]

Furthermore, Toynbee noticed there's always the consistent pattern for the growth of civilisations, with a creative minority leading a rearguard, sluggish, majority of the population.[169] Society, he said, works on mimesis, or imitation of behaviour, and development arises when the creative minority sets an excellent example by breaking new ground for the rest of the nation to follow. Social mimesis has to be effective to keep a society cohesive. Toynbee concluded that this pattern, whereby a strong creative leadership moulds a nation through an effective system of mimesis, constituted a fixed law of human nature and social growth. Just as nature works according to laws, so does history.[170]

For Toynbee, there are proven cycles of history: 'Certainly, in the movement of all these forces that weave the web of human history, there is an obvious element of recurrence.'[171] The key word here is 'recurrence'. Certainly, the great scholar had detected evidence of definite 'periodic repetitive movements'[172] but he took pains to point out that the process of civilisation was progressive, heading in a linear direction, rather than cyclical. That is why he found a rich diversity in the ways different societies grow but more uniform ways in which they disintegrate. That is, breakdowns follow a much more predictable process than development does. In fact, he found so much regularity in the way societies break down that he compared it to a rhythm in music: 'rout-rally-rout-rally-rout-rally-rout: three-and-a-half beats. This pattern is exemplified in the histories of several extinct societies...'[173]

The futurist must train his or her eye to see underlying patterns.

You could say that in Toynbee's view history moves forward in cycles or waves, rather than being a cycle itself. It has a rhythm he described as a 'series of successive cycles'.[174] History comprises the 'geneses and growths and breakdowns and disintegrations of human societies'.[175] There is an identifiable disintegration process as well as a growth process.[176]

These wave-like cycles of growth which push history onwards in a linear progression help us to foretell the future by reading or spotting them as they evolve. What gives us the right to do that?

What's important for our study is that the same causal structure that underpins the workings of nature runs through history. There is a golden chain of causation running through the universe and through the life of humanity. History, in other words, is just as causal as life itself.

Toynbee identified definite patterns of breakdown in human societies, in addition to his patterns of social growth: 'the nature of the breakdowns of civilizations can be summed up in three points: a failure of creative power in the minority, an answering withdrawal of mimesis on the part of the majority and a consequent loss of social unity in the society as a whole'.[177] The recurrent nature of these historic patterns suggests that similar causal factors are at work producing the same long-term effects.

Toynbee analysed why thirteen civilisations out of a total of the twenty-one which he studied had perished and why a further seven were in decline.[178] According to his model if a society is run by corrupt, self-interested and/or militaristic 'politicians' (and, one might add, where there are no towering leaders like Nelson Mandela to bring unity of vision, purpose and values to a divided society), such vacuums of governance will cause future social breakdown.

The margin between success and failure is thin since the same factors which make mimesis so effective – getting people to follow a vision as exemplified by its leaders – can bring about a downfall when the leaders are corrupted by their power, begin to believe in their own mythology, and start to use that process increasingly for their own advantage, leading eventually to a rebellion of the rank and file protesting against the abuse of power.[179]

The value of Toynbee's model is that it can be used not just to understand past failures and successes, but, more relevantly, to foretell future ones. For example, we could identify at which stage along the evolution of civilisation a society is and then come up with a diagnosis regarding the health of relations between rulers and ruled: 'the ultimate criterion and the fundamental cause of the breakdowns which precede disintegrations is an outbreak of internal discords through which societies forfeit their faculty of self-determination'.[180]

The thing to look for in the diagnosis is how estranged the minority leadership and its majority population are. Schisms of this nature, with widespread disenfranchisement, put a society on the road to dissolution. Using Toynbee's model, our diagnosis can be the basis for a causal prognosis.

It's the scientific method which makes it possible to progress from diagnosis to prognosis, just as a medical doctor often does. And it is the lawfulness of regular behaviour which provides the underlying justification for the prediction part of the analysis. Specifically, it's the patterns in behaviour over time which enable the behaviour of future cycles to be predicted within a time period.

Toynbee outlined both the sequence of events typical in phases of history and, where possible, the typical time frames: 'We have already found that, in the field of encounters between civilizations, the time-interval between the creation of an intelligentsia and its revolt against its makers has had an average length of about 137 years in a set of three or four examples; and it is not difficult to see how a concatenation of three or four generations might also determine the wavelength of a war-and-peace cycle.'[181]

Amid the destruction of the First World War, this iconic historian had asked himself a simple but deep question: why do civilisations die? It took him decades of study and thinking to find and publish the answer. In the sprawling work of scholarship that is *A Study of History*, he discovered 'cyclical movements in human history' moving forward like a wheel with 'repetitive circular motion', a process which he claimed was governed by laws of history.[182] There were laws at work both in the growth and in the decline of civilisations. He regarded it as historical fact that there's a great regularity and uniformity in the phenomena of social disintegration contrasting with a diversity and relative irregularity in the phenomena of social growth.[183]

Are there not economic laws just as there are laws of history? Certainly, there are well-documented regular cycles of boom and bust in capitalist economies and in business, analysed in pioneering studies by Kondratieff and Schumpeter. One of the many causal influences driving these cycles is the role of debt and risk in financial markets. There was too much debt and risk in the global financial system, originating in the sub-prime mortgage sector in the USA, leading up to the 2008 credit crisis. Were there any similarities in the instability preceding the stock market crash of 1929 and the subsequent Great Depression?

To find out, we turn now to John Kenneth Galbraith (1908–2006), former president of the American Economic Association, chairman of the Journal of Post Keynesian Economics and economic adviser to President John F. Kennedy. In the foreword to his 1954 book *The Great Crash 1929* he described the stock market crash of 1929 as the greatest cycle of speculative boom and collapse in modern times.

Galbraith established that all booms (and boomlets) have to end and that speculative bubbles are easy to puncture: 'when prices stopped rising – when the supply of people who were buying for an increase was exhausted – then ownership on margin would become meaningless and everyone would want to sell'.[184] He sees the behaviour of stocks as driven by human nature (undoubtedly one of the universal causal factors behind much of what happens in society). In particular, what lay behind the speculative bubble of 1929 was 'an inordinate desire to get rich quickly with a minimum of physical effort' coupled with a 'capacity for self-delusion'.[185] Paul M. Warburg of the International Acceptance Bank called for an end to unrestrained speculation in March 1929 predicting a general depression involving the entire country if the Federal Reserve did nothing.[186] The immediate cause of the crash of 1929, in other words, was unbridled stock market speculation and the cause of *that* was what Greenspan once called irrational exuberance. The good economic times of the roaring twenties – when, according to Galbraith, production and employment was high, prices were stable and wages were under control – fuelled the stock market boom, with corporate earnings growing and stock prices at competitive levels with good yields, and a culture of indulgence. However, the economic fundamentals were beginning to deteriorate and the overheated stock market was about to explode. A speculative boom is an accident waiting to happen.

In this classic case of boom followed by bust, Galbraith saw an underlying cause and effect process at work. The stock market, he explained 'is but a mirror which ... provides an image of the underlying or fundamental economic situation. Cause and effect run from the economy to the stock market, never the reverse. In 1929 the economy was headed for trouble. Eventually that trouble was violently reflected in Wall Street.'[187]

One of these economic factors which was changing at the time was the production cycle. Gailbraith explains: 'Production of industrial products, for the moment, had outrun consumer and investment demand for them... As a result they curtailed their buying, and this led to a cutback in production. In short, the summer of 1929 marked the beginning of the familiar inventory recession.'[188]

On Black Thursday, 24 October 1929, '12,894,650 shares changed hands, many of them at prices which shattered the dreams and hopes of those who owned them ... [the market] surrendered to blind, relentless fear.'[189] The financial carnage had begun. And the contagion of panic spread, with a 'chain reaction' of liquidations.[190] Investment trusts fizzled. Banks suffered irreparable losses. Fortunes vaporised, and 'The crash blighted the fortunes of many hundreds of thousands of Americans.'[191]

We all know the impact on American society was catastrophic. 'After the Great Crash came the Great Depression which lasted, with varying severity, for ten years. In 1933, Gross National Product (total production of the economy) was nearly a third less than in 1929. Not until 1937 did the physical volume of production recover to the levels of 1929, and then it promptly slipped back again. Until 1941 the dollar value of production remained below 1929. Between 1930 and 1940 only once, in 1937, did the average number of unemployed during the year drop below eight million. In 1933 nearly thirteen million were out of work, or about one in every four in the labour force. In 1938 one person in five was still out of work.'[192]

The crash, then, and all the misery it caused, was implicit in the speculative bubble of 1929 and in other declining economic factors. Here's one of the reasons why this is cyclical: 'Speculation ... is most likely to break out after a substantial period of prosperity, rather than in the early phases of recovery from a depression.'[193] In times of prosperity, that is, excess wealth, good savings and the accompanying mood of optimism themselves fuel the factors which lead, eventually, to an overheated economy. The terrible impacts of a crash linger in the collective memory and help to restrain irrational exuberance – but only for a time: 'The ensuing collapse automatically destroys the very mood speculation requires. It follows that an outbreak of speculation provides a reasonable assurance that another outbreak will not immediately occur. With time and the dimming of memory, the immunity wears off. A recurrence becomes possible. Nothing would have induced

Americans to launch a speculative adventure in the stock market in 1935. By 1955 the chances are very much better.'[194]

Under the surface change of economics, cycles are at work, driven by human and economic causes: 'The notion that the economy requires occasional rest and resuscitation has a measure of plausibility and also a marked viability.'[195]

In *A History of Economics* Galbraith discusses the potential role of foreknowledge in economics. He thought that a lot of the economic future was in the present but believed that forecasts themselves were 'inherently unreliable'.[196] He contended that 'many of the forces that initiate change cannot be predicted; they are outside the knowledge of economists'.[197] Nevertheless, he urged economists to try to form a picture of 'what in the past and the present in economics will be part of future history'[198] because 'the future can be seen in the present'[199] and 'The past, as we have seen ... actively and powerfully shapes not alone the present but the future...'[200]

The key to reading the future lies in understanding the cycles of history and nature. It's about identifying underlying causes driving these cycles.

But the cycle with the greatest influence on the long-term destiny of nations and humanity hasn't been discussed yet. I'm not referring to any of the cycles of history, sociology or economics discussed in this chapter.

The greatest cycle of all in determining the future of societies is demographic.

8
Demographics of destiny

'World population growth has already slowed dramatically over the last generation and is headed on course for absolute decline. Indeed, forecasts by the United Nations and others show the world population growth rate could well turn negative during the lifetimes of people now in their 40s and 50s.'

Phillip Longman,
The Empty Cradle (2004)

Population trends are a critical prognostic indicator for the long-term future of nations. They drive changes across a range of fields from economics and finances to politics, from sociology to international relations. Ultimately, they reveal the very health of nations and of humanity itself.

To the futurist, the quote above is a fearful one. Longman, a demographer and senior fellow at the New America Foundation, is telling us that population growth for humanity is likely to turn negative around mid-century. This means the world's total population size could start to decrease in absolute terms. If such a trend ever became irreversible, it would eventually lead to the extinction of the human race.

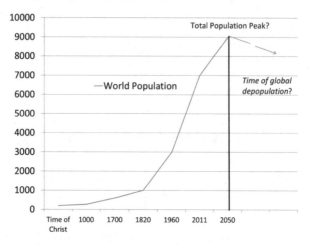

Figure 16: The rise of world population to its projected peak in 2050

Figure 16 indicates that the total human population may peak in 2050 at nine billion and thereafter decline year after year, decade after decade, generation after generation. It's not a comforting thought that population peak for the human race is probably just up ahead of us. Do we really want to be in decline as a species? Of course not. Yet, we seem to be slowly and steadily losing the appetite to procreate and reproduce our species at a robust rate.

It's not the long-feared population explosion that'll imperil us in the long term but Longman's population depletion scenario. We will fail to replace our numbers in successive generations and gradually become a dwindling population.

Visions of shrinking nations and families conjure up nightmarish scenarios of a declining world population. If sub-replacement fertility rates across the world continue compounding century after century it's a mathematical certainty that the human race will one day become extinct. By when will humans become an endangered species if current trends go on indefinitely?

Let's look at the facts of the matter and then paint a futurological picture of what kind of world would result from continued population decline. It's important to note that we're already seeing significant declines in birth rates right across the world, sometimes well below replacement levels, so this isn't science fiction here. The populations of major nations like Japan and Russia are already shrinking in size at worrying rates.

Coupled with this threat is the socioeconomic challenge of what Longman calls 'global population ageing'.[201] Societies in Asia, Europe and the Americas are turning grey and there are concerns about the drain on public expenditure and the loss of national productivity this ageing trend will entail. Population ageing will place added burdens on both government finances and the working generation. This affects the economy directly: 'There is a reasonably robust theory ... that suggests people accumulate wealth between the ages of 30 and 60 for retirement, after which they tend to save less or "dis-save".'[202]

We'll see in this chapter how demographic cycles underpin many economic and social cycles. Although cause and effect relations work strongly from the demographic domain to the economic realm, there's often a self-feeding loop between the two.

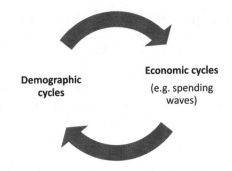

Demographic
cycles

Economic cycles
(e.g. spending
waves)

Figure 17: Loop between demographic and economic cycles

Population trends affect production and productivity, supply and demand, spending patterns, public finance and economic growth. Economic factors, in turn, affect populations while such factors as technology impact people's lives and habits. For example, birth-control pills have contributed to falling fertility. Products of the consumer society, such as televisions and fast foods, have created their own set of health problems from obesity to diabetes, while the rising economic costs of raising children drive down the birth rate even further. It could be argued that this has now become a feedback loop and is functioning as a vicious circle in the world.

In addition, falling living standards can further decrease the urge to bring children into a world with gloomy economic prospects.

Figure 18: Vicious circle of national decline

The scenario depicted in Figure 18 is actually happening in a country like Japan, once the second largest economy in the world, but now into its third decade of sluggish growth due to its twin curses of declining population and productivity, and population ageing.

Demographic trends are, by their nature, long term and far-reaching in their effects. Demographic data seldom lies. Rather, it provides a robust capacity for prediction: 'These predictions come with considerable certainty.'[203] Demographers know 'how many people will be over 65 in 2050, because those people have already been born'.[204]

When the causal relations stemming from demographic realities are mapped out, we realise that population trends do determine the future of a society in major ways. Whoever coined the evocative phrase 'demography is destiny', apparently paraphrasing the ancient saying 'character is destiny', came up with a winner.[205]

No wonder Benjamin Franklin was optimistic about the future of America given that in his time its birth rate was double that of Europe. Don't read Nostradamus, read demographic data.

Today, the position in America has been reversed and there are no grounds for any of Franklin's demographic optimism. Between 1990 and 2002, the crude birth rate in the US declined by 17 per cent: 'the last year in which white Americans had enough children to replace themselves was 1971'.[206] The future picture resulting from this population profile today is not so rosy with promise.[207]

What impact do demographic cycles have on society and on economic systems and performance? Longman establishes a link between the two fields of enquiry early in his landmark book *The Empty Cradle*: 'Capitalism has never flourished except when accompanied by population growth.'[208] Businesses, he says, go where populations are growing, not where they're declining. Why? Because there'll be more demand for their goods: 'More people create more demand for the products capitalists sell, and more supply of the labor capitalists buy.'[209] Here's the simple equation illustrating the loop between demographics and economics: 'Because of today's low birth rates, there will be fewer workers available in the future to produce the goods and services consumed by each retiree.'[210]

And here's the result for the economy: 'The working population of the United States essentially will wind up paying one out of every five dollars it earns just to support retirees, while simultaneously trying to finance more and more years of higher education...', creating financial disincentives for families to produce many children.[211]

A stagnant population, in other words, is likely to produce a stagnant economy. When there's depopulation, investment and business confidence eventually vanish, along with economic growth: 'Without population growth providing an ever increasing supply of workers and consumers, economic growth would depend entirely on pushing more people into the work force and getting more out of them each day.'[212]

It's not just economic momentum that gets lost when populations decline. The trend also brings about the depletion of a key resource of society: what is known as human capital. Investopedia explains human capital as follows: 'A measure of the economic value of an employee's skill set... The education, experience and abilities of an employee have an economic value for employers and for the economy as a whole... Economist Theodore Schultz invented the term in the 1960s to reflect the value of our human capacities. He believed human capital was like any other type of capital; it could be invested in through education, training and enhanced benefits that will lead to an improvement in the quality and level of production.'[213] Clearly, human capital is a major input for all growth and prosperity.

Longman is concerned that our current economic systems are exhausting the stock of human capital, pushing down the fertility rate and putting unsustainable economic demands on workers: 'When the economy demands more and more education from its workers, while providing them with neither the time nor the money to raise and educate their replacements in the next generation, the stock of human capital falls and is not easily renewed.'[214] An economic system, of 'mass consumption and mass production',[215] which does not properly compensate its population for child-rearing and parenting, and actually creates disincentives for these life-giving functions,[216] will tend to deplete its human stock.

If that system, at the same time, has to deal with a shrinking working-age population and a growing proportion of older people dependent on health care and pensions,[217] it's headed for trouble. Longman admonishes: 'a system that consumes more human capital than it produces must one day end'.[218]

It becomes a system that's eating itself.

Although skilled workers drive the revenue produced by businesses which, in turn, replenishes the tax base of a nation, our type of society does not invest in, or reward, the family unit responsible for nurturing the supply of the next generation of workers. Just as we're exhausting too rapidly the finite energy supplies of oil, gas and coal, so we're failing to secure the foundation for generating future human capital.

Longman has eloquently captured the twin threats to our common future of a below-replacement fertility rate and the erosion of the base of human capital. He argues that an economy which creates disincentives to have children, undercompensating parents and other caregivers for creating new human capital, is living beyond its means.[219]

Taking the above factors into account, how big a threat to the future is the depopulation bomb? There's the ultimate risk of long-term extinction to consider as well as the more immediate danger of a crippled world economy.

The core fact is that global fertility rates are half what they were in 1972. This is a disturbing reality, given that fertility rates are what keep the human race reproducing itself. The fall in global fertility is the key global problem to address in this century. Let's share the factual situation before digging down to the causes.

The following data together brings home the extent of this trend, bearing in mind that the replacement fertility rate is 2.1 children per woman and that at the start of the twentieth century, the global fertility rate was higher than five children per woman of child-bearing age:

- The world's population growth rate has fallen from 2 per cent p.a. in the late 1960s to just over 1 per cent today, and is predicted to slow further to 0.7 per cent by 2030 and then 0.4 per cent by 2050.[220]

- At present, 62 countries, making up almost half the world's population, have fertility rates at, or below, the replacement rate of 2.1, including most of the industrial world and Asian powers like China, Taiwan and South Korea.[221]

- Most European countries are on a path to population ageing and absolute population decline;[222] in fact, no country in Europe is demographically replacing its population.[223]

- 'If Europe's current fertility rate of around 1.5 births per woman persists until 2020, this will result in 88 million fewer Europeans by the end of the century.'[224]

- Spain has the lowest fertility rates ever recorded.

- Russia and most of the Balkans and Eastern Europe are facing a fall in the size of their populations of between 13 and 35 per cent in the next four decades, with China's starting to fall between 2030 and 2035, and Thailand's after about 2040.[225]

- Japan's fertility rate is 1.4 children per woman, one of the lowest.

- China's fertility rate is between 1.5 and 1.65.

- Mexico's fertility rate is below 2.5 children per woman.

- Cuba has one of the lowest fertility rates in the world.

- Italy, once the seat of the Roman Empire that ruled most of the known world, has a suicidally low fertility rate of 1.2.

- Turkey has a fertility rate of 2.32 children per woman.

- Since 1975, Brazil's fertility rate has dropped nearly in half to just 2.27 children per woman.[226]

- By mid-century China could lose 20 to 30 per cent of its population every generation.[227]

- By 2050, the median age of the world's population will be 38 years. In Europe this will be 47; in China, 45; in North America and Asia about 41.[228]

What is the scale of the population decline problem as these facts are absorbed? Longman explains: 'All told, some 59 countries, comprising roughly 44 percent of the world's total population, are currently not producing enough children to avoid population decline, and the phenomenon continues to spread. By 2050, according to the latest United Nations projections, 75 percent of all countries, even in underdeveloped regions, will be reproducing at below-replacement levels.'[229] Consequently, the world population could peak around 2050.[230]

What are the major causes of this population decline? In a nutshell, they are:

- The political rise of women, embracing the knowledge and skills needed to pursue professional careers, has led to a diminishment of the more traditional role of motherhood. Longman notes that a woman's educational level is the best predictor of how many babies she'll have.

- The effects of the birth-control pill.

- Smaller families are a feature of urban culture compared to agricultural communities.

- The economic disincentives for having children – who have now become a source of escalating health and educational costs and whose future revenue as workers goes into business profits and state coffers, rather than parents' bank accounts.[231]

- An ageing population has fewer women of reproductive age. People over 60 will increase from 673 million to 2 billion by 2050, while the over 80s will rise from 88 million to over 400 million by 2050.[232]

- A mass-consumer, market-driven individualistic culture, including the influence of television and its soap operas and reality shows, its advertising and its global role models, works against the traditional values of motherhood and family.[233]

- High abortion and divorce rates lead to fewer children being born.

These causes are deep-rooted, locked into history.[234] The economics of families has shifted in favour of smaller families in urban cultures and this driver of population decline is unlikely to be easily reversed. The greatest crisis of the twenty-first century will not be climate change or peak oil but population decline. If family size shrinks, the nation shrinks, along with its labour force, its tax base, its stock of human capital and, finally, its wealth and geopolitical influence on the world stage.

In addition to altering the face of economies and nations across the globe, these demographic trends will change the balance of global power. When demographer George Magnus speaks about the 'the old-age bulge of developed countries and the youth bulge of developing ones'[235] he's not sharing a dry scholarly fact. The implications of this simple statement are nothing short of revolutionary for international relations.

Just as the changing dynamics of a nation's natural resources, from energy to food and water, foretell its economic fortunes, so its underlying demographics are a robust predictor of its social and economic trajectory.

Business and investment follow the path of least resistance to growth potential. Ageing developed nations will need to compete with younger and more vigorous developing nations for future investment opportunities. Younger populations have a much better consumer profile than older populations, which means they are able to push up demand for products and services, something which is falling in older nations that simply don't buy goods on the scale of younger populations. Growing economic power quickly translates into enhanced international power and influence.

It does not seem far-fetched to foresee political power shifts in the world towards today's developing nations as their 'youth bulge' populations and economies grow on the back of increased demand for products and services while demand in ageing developed nations drops. Most Western countries, as well as China, have fertility rates below population replacement level.

As a futurologist, I believe demographics and resources (especially energy) are the two biggest determining causes of a nation's economic future. Futurology always moves from diagnosis to prognosis. Let's look at the Demography Future Radar. It's the crystal ball for humanity's future.

If you want to look into the medium- and long-term future of a nation, first look at its demographic future, especially when assessing how its demographic cycle is going to affect its future economy.

For example, let's look into the future demographics of two important nations, Russia and India. Russia is facing a depopulation bomb. It's estimated to lose between 13 and

35 per cent of its population size in the next four decades. In 1937 Russia had a population of 162 million and this has already fallen to 142 million, predicted to fall further to about 80 to 90 million by mid-century. Between 1937 and 2050, then, the country's population size could have halved. At a time when it's once again emerging as an energy giant, its demographics, ironically, are undermining its future prospects. The demographic challenge of halting depopulation will be complicated by the presence of an estimated 14.5 million Muslims in the country which may threaten unity and heighten ethnic tensions within its borders.

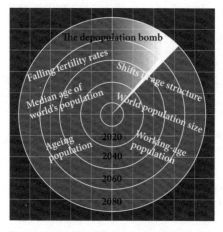

Figure 19: Radar of the demographic future
(radar illustration © Roman Sotola/123RF.COM)

Bad demographics like this can cause social problems in addition to economic deterioration. China's demographic gender profile, for example, is shockingly imbalanced, with an excess of males to the tune of about 40 million which, Magnus argues, is 'spawning a booming sex industry, a rising incidence of rape, and the abduction and sale of young girls as wives'.[236]

India, by contrast, has promising demographics and has been described as Asia's future America. Not only is the fertility rate at three children per woman but it has a relatively youthful population. On top of that, its growing economic power is in the services sector, where it is performing strongly in information technology, banking, finance, media, entertainment – all firmly in step with the Information Age. It is expected to surpass China's population by 2025.

For the world as a whole, though, the demographic prognosis is not good. In Magnus' words: 'birth rates have fallen well below the replacement rate of the population in many rich, and some poor, countries at a time when the age structure is shifting steadily toward older groups. With that comes the threat of economic decline and rising social tension.'[237]

Looking into the far future, demographically we're on a road to ultimate extinction. Says Longman: 'If human population does not wither away in the future, it will be because of a mutation of human culture.'[238] That is the most arresting comment I've ever read.

What demography teaches us is that in the long run any civilisation which takes women, marriage and the economics and ethics of the human family for granted is a doomed society.

Prognosis can help us to change bad policies, destructive values and practices and to reverse trajectories headed for destruction. It can save us time before it runs out for good.

But prognosis should follow proper professional methods. Otherwise, it could end up adding fuel to the fire.

9

A method for prognosis

'A method is required in order to search for the truth about things.'

René Descartes, *Discourse on Method for Guiding Reason and Searching for Truth in the Sciences* (1637)

Cycles of time, in which things behave in regular ways within specific periods of time, whether seasons, economic waves, human generations or product lifecycles, occur throughout nature and society. The study of time behaviour patterns of systems, entities and population groups provides the futurologist with a rational basis for prognosis. Prognosis is possible because things behave with sufficient regularity over time. The future is simply another phase of time.

But what step-by-step method should be followed in producing prognostic knowledge?

The core word in the quote above from the great scientific philosopher, René Descartes, is method. It derives from the Greek *methodos*, with *hodos* signifying 'way'. A method is the correct way to look for truth. I take a method to be a systematic procedure for developing new knowledge.[239]

In the space–time continuum, in which space and time are inseparable, all change happens in the time dimension. In this continuum, nothing is separate from time. So it makes sense to measure how things behave and change in, or across, time. Specifically, entities operate in typical cycles, or recurrent time trajectories.

In all science, observation of *current* behaviour leads to inductive conclusions about *recurrent* behaviour. Since recurrent behaviour is founded on regularity, and regularity can reflect universal laws and principles, it's important to assess the consistency of the induction about recurrent behaviour made within a framework of established theoretical knowledge.

In addition, systems thinking requires that we should contextualise the recurrent behaviour in question within a network of interdependent systems in nature and society. That's because the social world we observe exists on top of the physical world in a stack of interconnected realities, all within 4D space–time. Space and time are intertwined, but so are nature and society. This is a deeply networked world.

It's also dynamic, subject to change. Chapter 7 showed that as things change over time they form time shapes or patterns of behaviour. In particular, cycles of existence have been examined in nature and history.[240] It's useful to visualise these patterns of time cycles as part of the process leading to prognosis.

For example, one of the best known time patterns is the bell shape. Figure 20 shows the Hubbert production curve.

Hubbert used this bell-shaped pattern to predict both the peak of US oil production and global oil production decades ahead. In economics, wave patterns of 'boom and bust' are recurrent. Kondratieff discovered long waves of economic growth and decline in capitalist economies over time periods of around fifty to sixty years.

There are many cycles in economics, including production cycles, business cycles and stock market cycles. American economist Robert Ayres considered the key to cycles of economic growth to be costs of power and energy and the associated efficiency ratio of conversion of energy into work and production.[241] He believed he'd identified the engine driving economic growth.

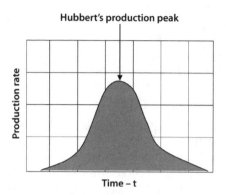

Figure 20: Hubbert's bell-shaped cycle of production of any exhaustible (finite) resource. Shaded area = ultimate cumulative production. (Reproduced from *Knowing our Future – the startling case for futurology*.)

Henry Ludwell Moore (1869–1958), who pioneered the field of econometrics in the USA, looked for the law behind the rhythmic ebb and flow of economic life, its alternating periods of growth spurts and depressions. He concluded it was largely dependent at that time on agricultural production which, in turn, was affected by weather patterns and, in particular, by rainfall. Moore saw cause and effect relationships between annual rainfall, supply of crops and consequent prices.

Moore was deeply intrigued by the interrelationships between cycles of crops and their weather patterns, cycles of activity in industry and cycles in general prices: 'a rising yield in the crops would lead to an increase in the volume of trade, an increase in the demand for producers' goods, an increase in employment, a rise in the demand curves for crops, with the final result of a rise in general prices ... the congruence of the two rhythmical movements of crop yield and general prices is so close as to justify the inference that the one series is the cause of the other'.[242]

He formulated the following economic law: 'The rhythm in the activity of economic life, the alternation of buoyant, purposeful expansion with aimless depression, is caused by the rhythm in the yield per acre of the crops; while the rhythm in the production of the crops is, in turn, caused by the rhythm of changing weather which is represented by the cyclical changes in the amount of rainfall. The law of the cycles of rainfall is the law of the cycles of the crops and the law of Economic Cycles.'[243] He described this interrelationship as a sequence of causation.

As with all laws, they permit predictions due to their likely recurrences in future: 'it is possible to predict the prices of the crops from the yield per acre with the same precision with which prices may be predicted from the demand curves ... the productivity of the soil is as closely related to the prices of crops as the supply of the commodity is to the same prices'.[244]

It's fascinating, as Ayres and Moore showed in their work, figuring out what drives cycles in economics and society. Today, US economic forecaster Harry S. Dent, Jnr, uses demographic trends to predict spending waves and associated booms and busts.

Another familiar cycle in business and economics is the S-curve time pattern.

The S-curve growth cycle is typical of technologies, products and services which make an impact on the market and then are gradually superseded by innovations which beat them for cost, convenience and effectiveness. At its heart, the S-curve is the measurement of a trajectory. It's a time pattern.

Other time patterns would be plotting simple increases and decreases over time.

The most common time pattern of all is the lifecycle itself. Things have a lifespan of a specific duration, with a beginning, a high point of existence, then a period of decline, leading to extinction. These are time-bound trajectories of development for all living and existing things.

Figures 20 to 22, then, show how entities and systems can behave over time as we trace their changing positions, performance, etc. When these recognisable patterns or shapes are part of natural and social regularities, it becomes possible to watch their predetermined courses in advance in order to prefigure their futures. The more durable and therefore repeatable the cycle we're observing is, the more clearly we'll be able to see the future motion, or behaviour, of things in their cycles. Things in nature and society are truly locked into their time cycles.

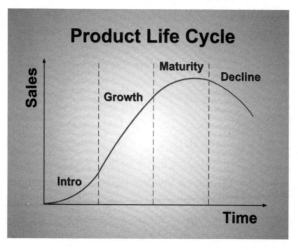

Figure 21: S-curves

For example, the solar system has its gravitational orbits which are durable over millennia. As Galileo, Copernicus, and Newton discovered, the behaviour of planets and moons in the solar system is orbital. Earth, as we know, has its cycles of day and night and of the passing of the seasons. Our own human cycle is universal. These are all very durable cycles. Therefore they can be used as a basis for prognosis or prediction. In the previous chapter, demographic trends were shown to influence economic cycles of consumption and production. Time patterns are an excellent prognostic tool.

In the FutureFinder system described in Chapters 11 to 13, individuals, organisations and systems can get onto a better trajectory of the future by working on a range of specific factors which can influence their development in a causal manner.

It's the trajectory that counts, after all, since everything has its own cycle of existence, and passes along a course in pursuit of a direction in which it is headed. Cycles and trajectories form patterns which persist into the future.

These cycles are the invisible tracks along which organisms and entities move in regular patterns. These repeatable, durable cycles provide the blueprints for the prediction of future movement. Regularity remains the basis of prediction. And life throughout the universe is pretty predictable.

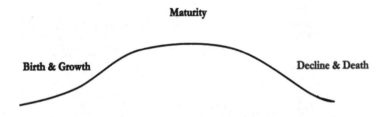

Maturity

Birth & Growth

Decline & Death

Figure 22: The universal lifecycle

Such cycles are periodic. Time, as part of the space–time fabric, operates in a highly organised universe with its properties and its laws of motion, gravity and energy. Time performs its work with the same degree of organisation displayed everywhere else. That fact, to me, is the origin of time's regularity. Time's regularity, in turn, allows us to evolutionise the study of behaviour as a platform for prognosis – that is, to place things within their time trajectories. To evolutionise means to measure something's long-term change and growth patterns (progress or decline) within definite time periods.

This step enables the projection of a future path of development as part of preconstructing the future. Reconstruction of past behaviour, in other words, leads the way to preconstruction of future behaviour.

A step-by-step method for systematic thinking lies at the heart of the scientific revolution which created our modern age. This method may now be applied to a study of the future to create an infinitely useful body of foreknowledge. There's nothing exotic about it, either: futurology is based on the same causal model behind all scientific thought and prediction.

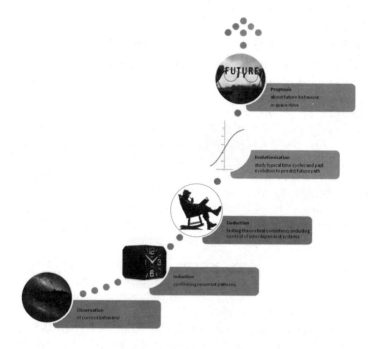

Figure 23: Building prognosis the scientific way

Note that the prognostic method outlined in Figure 23 moves in its logical ascension from simple to complex, and from known to unknown, as recommended by Descartes.[245]

A method follows a step-by-step procedure. Descartes recommended beginning with the most simple propositions and gradually working up through induction and intuition to more complex truths: 'In order to distinguish the simplest things from those that are complex and to search for them in an orderly way, one should notice what is most simple in each sequence of things in which we have directly deduced some truths from others, and how all the others are more, or less, or equally distant from the most simple item.'[246] Application of the method progresses along a 'long chain of inferences' and follows a 'continuous movement of thought'.[247]

In the method of prognosis recommended here, as visualised in Figure 23, the futurist uses observation, induction, deduction, contextualisation and evolutionisation in their right order.

As one of the co-inventors of the philosophy of science, Descartes was not being overly academic. For him, scientific knowledge had to be useful to 'human needs', leading to a mastery of nature, while also fostering human wisdom.[248] Knowledge, Descartes said, aids 'the discovery of an infinite number of devices that would enable us to enjoy, without any effort, the fruits of the earth and all the goods we find there, but, also, especially, for the preservation of health which is undoubtedly the foremost good and the foundation for all the other goods of this life'.[249] As Hans Reichenbach, another major scientific philosopher, stated: 'knowledge is indispensable for the control of objects of our environment'.[250]

The true beauty of the scientific method is its universality and flexibility, applicable to all kinds of subject matter.[251] This should include study of the future. Descartes was excited about the potential of the method he'd helped to create: 'as long as one always observes the order required to deduce them from each other, there cannot be anything so remote that it cannot eventually be reached nor anything so hidden that it cannot eventually be uncovered'.[252]

Systematic knowledge of the future of the world is possible due to the significant degree of regularity in the behaviour of nature and society. This book attempts to uncover the hidden order of the future, located in its causal structure which is entrenched in the present.

Scientific knowledge of the future would enable humanity to increase inventiveness, to become proactive in problem solving, to heighten our natural gift for anticipation and to reduce the frequency of social crises, including limiting damage from natural disasters.

Finding this hidden order would result in increased control over the world. Is there anybody out there who would disagree that this power is desperately needed?

10
Modelling the hidden order of the future

'For we are founding a real model of the world.'
Francis Bacon, *Novum Organum* (1620)

For most of humanity, the future is still the unseen unknown. It's uncharted territory. It's the Great Unknown.

But the future is categorically *not* the Great Unknowable. For those who understand prognosis, especially the role of causation in the universe, it has a hidden order we can grasp. As detectives of time, scientific futurists can painstakingly piece together the puzzle of tomorrow's world.

And if the future does have a hidden nature, like the cosmos does, like history does, it would be possible to model it.

The invisible order of the future searched for in this book is located in time itself.

While Spengler spoke of the logic of time, Hume praised time as an ordering principle. This great philosopher described both space and time as 'the manner or order in which objects exist'.[253] Time, for example, being itself successive, one moment always following after another, establishes the sequence of processes and events: 'Tis a property inseparable from time, and which in a manner constitutes its essence, that each of its parts succeeds another, and that none of them, however contiguous, can ever be co-existent ... every moment must be distinct from, and posterior or antecedent to another.'[254]

Processes happen in successive phases, as do events. That means time orders them into their sequence. Hume uses succession as a synonym for time,[255] seeing this quality as its essence. If time is an ordering principle for all processes and events, if it produces order for the objects of the universe, as Hume suggested, then it must have order in its very nature.

The future is part of the order of time, through the principle of the continuity of time. We see this continuity at work in evolutionary and causal processes.

Let's think about how everything, including our lives, flows into the future in this structured continuity and sequence of time.

It seems true that while the past pushes us from behind, with its causal and evolutionary processes, the future, by contrast, seems to pull us forward from the front. We feel ourselves to be continuously inside the tides of time. We are creatures of time. We flow into the future.

Imagine, for a moment, that you're standing at the finishing line of a 400-metre race at an athletics meeting. Let's say you're a top sports journalist and you know all about the runners taking part, including their average times for this distance, their worst and best times, and their recent form, current state of mind and fitness, etc. Armed with this information, you'll be able to look down the track before the race has begun and predict fairly accurately how it will unfold. You'll be able to conjure up in your mind a foreshadow of the future. You would picture seeing the race happening on the tracks leading up to the finishing line. The more pre-race information you have, the more accurate your prediction will be.

In a sense, during this mental exercise, you'd be viewing things from the vantage point of the future, looking back on the movement from present into future. You'd witness the athletes flowing into the future down the tracks mapped out for them.

Armed with foreknowledge, you'd have stepped ahead of the present and then looked back on the future coming towards you. From the perspective of the present, you'll experience the push of the past and the pull of the future as the athletes are literally propelled by time along their tracks, almost as if there's an invisible power cord stretching from the horizon behind them, passing through them and leading beyond the horizon ahead.

The athletes have purposes and goals both for this event and for their future careers. These plans are positioned in the future: they exert a force like a 'pulling' action from the front. At the same time, their skills, knowledge, training and experience are part of the past 'pushing' them ahead. Other causal factors are at work, too, in this push effect, such as motivations, moods, perhaps something inspirational their coaches may have said before the race. It is in this sense that time seems to propel us into the future.

In sum, while causes push life into the future, purposes pull it with incredible invisible power into the future.

Figure 24: Athletes propelled by the push of the past
and the pull of the future
(© jameschipper/123RF.com)

One of the reasons we can step into the future like this in mental time travel is that human activity is purposive, geared towards the attainment of set goals. Aristotle believed that everything had a built-in purpose for its existence. He was right: purposes (which are located in the future) determine behaviour to an extraordinary degree. If you know the purposes, you know the future behaviour that will be directed towards attaining them. Purpose dictates behaviour. The will to purpose is probably the deepest human urge of all. Without purpose and meaning, we'd be lost. As creatures of time, we're essentially goal-seeking beings needing meaning almost as much as we need water and food.

Human meaning is about finding a trajectory into a future in which our built-in purposes can find fulfilment.

Time, then, is not just the medium of causal change. It's the medium of physical processes pushing towards their built-in purposes. In that sense, Spengler was right in saying that time has a logic, Hume was right that time is an ordering principle and Aristotle was right that everything has a defining ontological purpose.

Figure 25: The push and pull into the future
(© michaeldb/123RF.com)

We find the hidden order of the future by studying the nature, principles, effects and processes of time. We can model the causal influences from the past and present. We can study and see the cycles of time. We can witness the orderly progression of the present into the future through a sequence. In Figure 25, there are both pushing forces and a pulling force. This image represents how the past pushes life forward while the future pulls it to add propulsion. A combination of causes and purposes lead us into the future. Both causes and purposes are knowable through the methods of science and logic.

Imagine being at a waterfall where you're admiring the power of the cascade of water. Then picture yourself moving downstream further below the waterfall to the river mouth, perhaps a few miles away. As you go, you observe the changes of direction and flow patterns of the river. From this new position downstream, you could plot in reverse the progress of the water making its way from the waterfall. You know the river always heads towards its destination in the same direction, following the same course. Over the ages it has worn a pattern in the ground which it follows and which you observed as you moved towards the mouth of the river. The river has a time pattern. Its motion from the waterfall to the river mouth can be anticipated because it's a regular motion following a well-worn course. The river's path is inevitable. If you go back to the waterfall, you could anticipate how the water will behave as it flows downstream.

The fact that there are so many well-trodden paths which life simply follows points to another 'squeeze' effect produced by time. Let's visualise how things progress from the present to the future. For the purposes of this next illustration, try to see the present time as a funnel.

Think of all possibilities which might exist in this present time, both for you and for entities around you. Then think of all the decisions that are made and actions that are taken which produce single outcomes as they are filtered through time to set in motion a new single course of action.

What were once a whole bunch of choices, options and possibilities have now been funnelled into one outcome in one future. Particles may be able to be in different locations at one time but people, entities and systems only have one future, not many futures; one path, not many paths; one position at a time, not many positions. The bizarre behaviour of particles at the level of quantum physics is not mirrored at the macroscopic level at which reality takes place for humans and the entities of our world. Unlike particles, people cannot be in two places at one time. It makes no difference that things seem to get scrambled in quantum physics. What's important for social knowledge is how things behave at our everyday, macroscopic level.

Figure 26: The funnel of the present, in which many possibilities turn into one future

If you look at Figure 26, you notice everything gets squeezed into one vast, evolving space–time (the funnel) and then comes out along one trajectory only. We've seen that life is given one physical direction only, which is forwards. This makes us by nature directional beings, designed to be forward-thinking.

Directions are very significant. They give us destinations. They influence everything we do.

Time is directional, as the funnel analogy suggests. All change happening inside the time funnel obeys the laws and limits of nature.

These laws were discovered through a superhuman effort over many centuries by great scientific thinkers such as Aristotle, Descartes, Bacon, Copernicus, Galileo, Kepler,

Newton, Poincaré, Einstein, Reichenbach, Watson, Crick and Stephen Hawking. The laws govern the whole of space–time in which we exist, including how gravity, motion and energy work. These canonical scientific thinkers attempted to prove how the world works and of what material it's made.

The universe of all possibilities gets continuously shaped and moulded into one, and only one, final product, and that is the world we see evolving around us. Figure 26 illustrates that space–time, our home, is a funnel through which everything passes as part of one living, unfolding history of the world. Think of the funnel as a set of laws everything must obey, including the law of causation moulding actions and changes.

So if futurists – or any thinkers – change their position in time, placing themselves at a definite point in the future, they'll be able to look back at what's going to happen. Things follow their evolutionary paths, trajectories from past to future, while conforming to nature.

Since time always turns into the future, never going backwards, it should be possible to watch that process happen – just like the sports journalist standing at the finishing line of the race track and forming a picture of how the race will unfold before it begins.

Physicists have shown us that things are passing through time – ageing – even when they are standing still. We do see the effects in the material world of this ageing process, this passage through time. In fact, we're travelling into the future even when sleeping. The car parked in the garage at night continues to travel through time though the engine is switched off. It will show the signs and effects of ageing as surely as human faces do – rust, fading colours, worn tyres, etc.

We time-travel into the future, mentally positioning ourselves there, and then look back to watch the future unfold.

Francis Bacon described knowledge evocatively as the 'image of existence'.[256] In prognosis, we need to turn vague foreshadows of the future into structured images and real models of the future. Yes, we can foresee the future in that it is foreshadowed in the present. But its hidden order needs to be unveiled through systematic investigation, piecing together the puzzle, piece by piece, until the foreshadows are turned into lifelike high-resolution pictures or 'images of existence' in the sense of Bacon's knowledge.

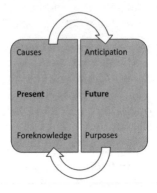

Figure 27: Interaction between present and future

In Figure 27, foreknowledge is produced by understanding the causes which enhance our ability to anticipate, while the purposes we strive towards, in turn, increase our stock of foreknowledge.

Foreknowledge begins as an interpretation of foreshadowing – the shadows cast backwards by the future as we anticipate and imagine what's going to happen next. We may get a premonition. Either way, the detective of time systematically pieces together the future.

The present is immersed in time: the past and the future. Nothing can escape the deep continuity of time. But mere subjective responses to foreshadows of the future are never going to be enough. Premonitions and anticipation are typically subjective. For prognosis, a thorough analysis of the future is required to identify the future effects of causes, the purposes that drive things forward, the cycles of time which allow us to plot future trajectory changes.

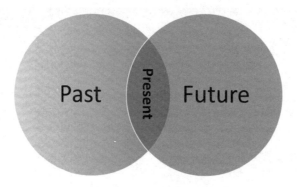

Figure 28: Foreshadows of the future and memories shadow the present

It is only through scientific knowledge, developed according to scientific methods, that we can build effective models for prognosis. Kant wrote that 'Method is procedure according to principles.'[257]

Once the correct methods have been used to generate prognostic knowledge we can use the same underlying principles to construct predictive models. This kind of predictive modelling happens in various disciplines. For example, we know NASA uses high-resolution global atmospheric modelling to study changing weather within Earth's climate system. The renowned space agency's Goddard Earth Observing System Model (GEOS-5) can simulate worldwide weather patterns (see Figure 29). Climate modelling is used for anticipating weather and climate patterns.

Higher level winds are colour-coded by speed with red indicating fast speeds. This kind of simulation was produced by a computer model which represents the Earth's atmosphere, with inputs including sea-surface temperatures and various surface emissions, from industrial sources and aerosols to volcanoes.

Models like this can paint pictures of the world's expected behaviour because they are based on well-established, recurrent characteristics of the system they represent. Scientific models must be based on laws which, in turn, describe regularities.

Figure 29: Images of global wind patterns produced by GEOS-5 simulation
on the Discover supercomputer (NASA Center for Climate Simulation;
Source: William Putman/NASA Goddard Space Flight Center)

The models are constructed by outlining the factors which drive regular behaviour. These factors are normally given weighting according to their influence. Data from recurrent past occurrences have been fed into the model to enable it to predict future behaviour.

Modelling the future is no different. In the next chapter, a model called FutureFinder, which has software programmes for individuals, organisations and nations, will be introduced.

A good analogy for making a model of the future is constructing a jigsaw without having any picture on the top of the puzzle box to use as a reference point. At first, the jigsaw-puzzlers – the futurists – have hundreds of isolated pieces (facts, data, information, ideas, intuitions) scattered in all directions on the table. They have little or no idea of the picture they'll end up constructing. Slowly, pieces which match are joined, completing certain areas of the puzzle. This work requires detailed comparative analysis of what each piece represents and how it might fit together with other pieces. As they assemble pieces in several areas, they start to think about what kind of picture the completed sections will make as a whole. When an unfolding pattern falls into place, they form a concept of the puzzle's subject matter. Their aim is to form a detailed vision of some developing future. The pieces of the future fit together in a cause and effect pattern.

Jigsaw-puzzlers progress from a study of individual pieces and how they connect to constructing sections which themselves link into an interconnected pattern. They create order from chaos by spotting regularities in the apparently random scattered pieces. There are patterns within patterns which form part of one broad picture. They look for the hidden causal order.

The key to this sort of inductive thinking is systematic observation leading to the identification of patterns or the discovery of persistent regularities. That's why this approach may also be defined as: 'the inference of a general law from particular instances'.[258] In the case of a jigsaw-puzzler, his or her reasoning would be expressed something like this: 'These pieces have similar colours and shapes so I will put them into one pile where I'll test if they actually fit into one another as it seems likely they will. If they do fit, it'll prove they belong together in a permanent relationship in the picture I am forming.'

The logical movement in induction is always from particular to general. It's also a matter of progressing from the known and seen (jigsaw pieces) to the unseen unknown (how the pieces fit together). Descartes insisted on moving from the simple to the complex.

Knowledge of the future is based primarily on this kind of induction. Futurists move from the observed known, in the present and past, to the unseen unknown of the future. They do this by identifying regular behaviours which are considered persistent or generally applicable. The explanations as to why the behaviour is regular in the first place will indicate how strong the relationships between the factors involved really are.

Since they start with so few knowns and so many unknowns, these jigsaw-puzzlers without a picture need to employ systematic logic to complete their task. From an inauspicious starting position they must derive definite conclusions about the future, and they use the powerful tool of induction to do this. After all, it's the best method for producing knowledge ever invented.

Our future is not a set of disconnected pieces lying on a table. The pieces fit together. Why wouldn't they? For they go together in a cause-and-effect structure.

The hidden structure of the future under the surface of infinite change has been pictured as a causal set of processes pushing us from the past, combined with the inherent force of purposes pulling us along. Let's model these processes for individuals, organisations and nations. Let's build and model the puzzle pictures of our future.

11

Finding the future for individuals

'For as there is much of the past that is in the present, so also there is much of the present that will be in the future...'

John Kenneth Galbraith, *A History of Economics – The Past as the Present* (1991)

How much would you pay to find your future? What's it worth to you to put yourself more firmly on a positive trajectory into the next phases of your life? How connected and invested are you in your future?

To me, the path that's chosen is everything. It's mission-critical for humans to have direction and purpose. It's just as important to face the right direction in time as it is to go in the right direction to get to a physical destination.

It should be a human right to have a future. To be without a future is a recipe for depression, if not desolation. Futurelessness breeds disorder.

Here is offered a science of the future to help you find your rational, purpose-driven destiny. Science has developed the best model for explaining how the real world works – the one you actually live in – using shared, evidence-based knowledge accumulated over centuries through patient observation and logic.

I recommend a rational approach to your future. Thankfully, I outgrew both pessimism and optimism a few years ago. I look at the future through scientific eyes, that is, making fact-based assessments and looking for cause and effect relations, taking responsibility for the causes I myself set in motion.

I enjoy being in the flow of time; I love 4D vision; I find existence within space–time to be a rich, experiential world. I look at all the surfaces of continuous changes, like light falling into the facets of a diamond to give scintillation and I see, as in an X-ray, the abiding structures and hidden order of the future.

A scientific approach to our future makes for better understanding of what lies ahead. It enables me to review what plans I should put in place, assessing what trajectory I'm on and what I need to change, adjust, modify or shift. All things, including you and I, are on an evolutionary path. By becoming aware of causal influences, and reviewing goals and purposes, we'll gain better control of the forces and conditions shaping our future.

Do you wish to develop a better understanding of your future and exert more control over its production?

In the previous chapter, it was argued that the future, like nature and history, has a hidden order we can learn to read as a decoded language. This fact has implications for individuals, organisations and nations.

It's my wish that every person should become better acquainted with, and connected to, the future. So I developed a model, programmed in software, called FutureFinder – one for individuals, one for organisations and one for nations.

The aim of FutureFinder for individuals is to guide them into a more positive future. The system identifies key causal factors of the future.

FutureFinder doesn't pretend there's a perfect future. We're flawed beings in a flawed world but we can work on progression even if perfection is out of reach on this side of the grave. I'd rather be progressing than stagnating or retrogressing. Progression is the goal of study of the future.

Recall for a moment the analogy of the sports journalist watching the athletes running the 400-metre race (see Figure 24). We saw then that purposes pull us towards the future. Some of these purposes are built in, part of who we are, while others can be formulated, such as life goals, career goals and financial goals, as well as more short-term goals. These goals and missions become causal in their impacts (plans and actions have consequences).

As an individual, you're being pushed (by causes) and pulled (by purposes) into the future. By becoming aware of these two forces of the future, you will gain greater control over what your life is becoming.

In the FutureFinder system, thirty future factors are arranged on a scale of importance according to the role they play in driving and determining our future. Each of these thirty factors, weighted according to relative causal influence, in keeping with the scientific theory of the future developed in this book, needs to be evaluated by the user on a scale of one to ten. The weighted scores can be plotted onto the continuum of progression illustrated in Figure 30. It contains three stages, namely, optimisation of the future (progression), sub-optimisation of the future or, at worst, heading in the wrong direction entirely (retrogression).

Note that the ultimate positive condition for your future is described in Figure 30 as 'optimal destiny', not perfection. I believe that dynamic equilibrium is the best condition for all things, people and systems, in which balance and order are attained but not at the expense of continuous growth.

That's because we can never be static in a cosmos that's in perpetual motion. In space–time, in which everything exists, even while we're sleeping we're still travelling through time (by ageing and changing). The idea is to stay ahead of change in this fast-moving world by being positive and proactive. The idea is to move with the motion of the space–time in which we live. That's why although I love balance and order, it has to be dynamic, not static. Static conditions will always be overtaken by change, since change is continuous and irreversible.

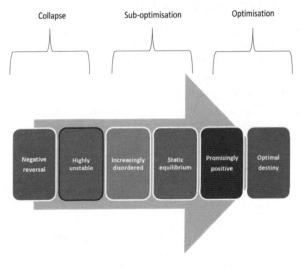

Figure 30: Continuum of progression for individuals

The opposite of such statis is progression. Accordingly, progression is the goal of the FutureFinder system.

I urge you to be future-facing from this day forward. The universe, and the time that orders the sequence of everything in it, both point in one direction only: forwards. So it makes sense to point in the same direction as the universe. That's the first step towards dynamic equilibrium.

It's important to use FutureFinder periodically to stay conscious of the future, encouraging you to keep making adjustments to your trajectory, to your plans, assessing the causal factors and purposes over which you've got some measure of control.

The objective behind the scoring procedure is to confront and evaluate a person's current historical trajectory honestly and objectively, to provide some quantification as a measurement. Changes can then be made where it matters most in order to pre-empt future deterioration. The quantification aspect is an important discipline to counterbalance our natural tendencies to be biased and subjective about ourselves, not easily admitting to weak areas or even failures.

Each factor in FutureFinder for individuals gets a score determined as follows:

Score	Scale of score	Meaning
1–2	Low score	Factor performing poorly with disastrous effects
3–4	Low score	Factor performing negatively with harmful effects
5–6	Medium score	Factor performing moderately with neutral effects
7–8	High score	Factor performing strongly with positive effects
9–10	High score	Factor performing dynamically with multiple beneficial effects

Table 2: Scoring system for FutureFinder

The thirty factors of FutureFinder provide a foundation for the future. Most of these future factors are within the individual's control. Even in the case of those which aren't, it's important to work on compensating for them through extra efforts on other, related, factors. The idea is to stimulate people to work hard on their continuous progress, dumping pessimism and optimism as subjective, mood-based approaches to the future, hangovers from the highly conflicted twentieth century. They're infections of the mind for which the scientific method is the only antidote. Short-termism is a disease and prognostic thinking is its cure.

Using the system should have the indirect benefit of inculcating a rational approach to the future. Individuals are encouraged to be as objective as possible. Each of their assessments for the thirty factors should be a rational judgment based on evidence, observations and reasons, never on guesswork.

An additional by-product of using the system is that it will teach the discipline of looking at the future holistically from all angles, not just from one or two angles arising from immediate issues and moods. The system is designed to give prominence to the overall cumulative effect of all the indicators when considered together. This reflects the idea that the individual's future is produced by multiple factors from dimensions like finances, health, genetics, education and background. The future factors are each influences on the formation of the future in conjunction with all the other factors. Bear in mind, too, that general background conditions, in addition to specific causes, can play a shaping role in the unfolding future.

What's true is that individuals can and should determine their future within the world they live in with all its multiple influences. What the FutureFinder system can do is highlight whether or not they are on track for a positive, negative or sub-optimal future, to find out whether they are in progression or retrogression.

The results of a FutureFinder scoring will identify areas where an individual is progressing and others where he or she is falling short in building a good, optimal future.

There's an inherent goodness in the concept of progression. It's yours to take hold of, invest in and work on in order to shape your destiny more clearly.

12

Finding the future for organisations

'Each successful Business Idea for the future has at its core an original entrepreneurial invention, underpinned by a new and unique insight about how this organisation can interact with the world.'
Kees van der Heijden, *Scenarios – the Art of Strategic Conversation* (2005)

Businesses, and other types of organisations, are systems. The word 'organisation' is a core concept of civilisation. It's derived from the Latin *organum* meaning instrument or tool. An organisation may be viewed as a form of conceptual technology. Scenario strategist Kees van der Heijden stresses the need for new 'Business Ideas' to give organisations a fresh presence in the world.

Where would humanity be today without tools, without technology? And the ultimate technology is, of course, the system. The organisation is the most important social technology. For NASA, as well as for all organisations, failure is not an option. There is too much at stake: wealth, jobs, reputations and the whole social order.

What role can the future play in keeping organisations fresh and effective? First, as systems, they need to face in the right direction in order to progress.

An organisation is defined as a body of people with a particular purpose, whether a business, government department or NGO. Organising means arranging in a systematic way.[259] Systems are so important and so universal that a powerful new interdisciplinary science called systems science,[260] based on systems thinking, has evolved over the last few decades.

The word 'system',[261] referring to how a set of interconnected parts operates, performs or behaves together as one functioning whole, has its roots in the Greek word *sustema,* from *sun* (meaning 'with') and *histanai* (meaning 'set up'). Why do we need to understand systems behaviour? The cosmos is made up of systems. Nature is made up of systems. Society is made up of systems. Even households operate through systems and sub-systems. Our bodies are systems. And most social, political and organisational problems are systemic in nature.

Systems have the following defining characteristics:

- Purposive – they exist only for specific and clear purposes and functions.

- Organised – their parts must work together cohesively in order to achieve their aims.

- Efficient – to survive and compete effectively in the long run, while producing the results required of them, they need to ensure a sustainable balance between their inputs and outputs.

- Intelligent – they continuously process information, both internal and external, to ensure they self-correct, adapt to change and develop.

Since physics has shown that time faces forwards only, I would add a fifth characteristic: systems need to be future facing.

Using a motor vehicle as an analogy of a system, let's show how these five characteristics of systems work.

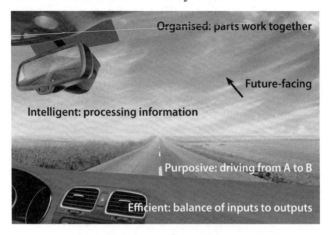

Figure 31: The five characteristics of systems
(photo © Carmen Steiner/123RF.COM)

The system in Figure 31 is on the open road, which represents its normal operating environment. What are the vehicle's five key features?

- The car is purposive: it must take its occupants to their destination.

- The car is organised: every part, from the tyres to the gears, functions as one unit.

- The car is efficient: it must achieve its goal with good fuel consumption and minimal stoppages or disruptions.

- The car is intelligent: its driver has the windscreen and rear-view mirror to receive external information (e.g. weather, approaching cars) as well as the dashboard for processing internal information (fuel level, speed, etc.).

- The car is future facing: its journey has been planned.

Notice the connection between purpose and the future. Things are designed with built-in purposes. These purposes are intelligent. In addition, new goals are continuously formulated for systems. According to the causal approach to the future developed in this book, these goals and purposes become causal influences on the system, 'pulling' it into the future (see Figures 24 and 25 in Chapter 10). As the saying goes, be careful what you wish for. Plans and purposes have a strong influence on the future.

In the FutureFinder system for organisations, the following future trajectory is used for assessing where an organisation finds itself on a continuum ranging from being an optimal organisation to collapsing.

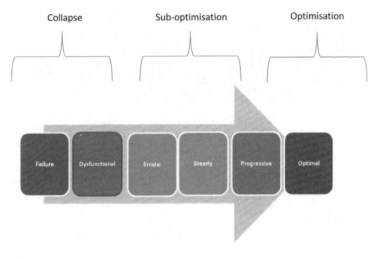

Figure 32: Finding the future for organisations

Since systems are purposive and intelligent, it's obvious that the core of any system is its ethos, its governing principles, its purposes, the reason for its existence. In the scoring system to determine where on the trajectory in Figure 32 any given organisation lies, future factors to do with ethos are weighted strongly as significant determinants of the future.

Does the organisation have a strong ethos by which it lives or dies? Ethos here covers the following elements: vision, mission, strategy, corporate governance, transparency, integrity and accountability as well as the culture of the organisation, including whether or not it promotes and nurtures innovation and creativity, backed up by an R&D function.

Globally, we've already entered an 'innovate or die' economy. Think of how quickly technologies and products can become obsolete.

Figure 33: Innovate or die: the scrap heap of obsolete technologies

To counteract the dire fate of being overtaken by changes that threaten the usefulness of a company's products and services, it is necessary to keep the concept of future-proofing in mind. The New Oxford Dictionary of English defines this as 'unlikely to become obsolete' while the Macmillan Dictionary explains it as follows: 'something that is future-proof will not stop being used because it has been replaced by something newer and more effective'. Using the FutureFinder system on a quarterly basis should enable organisations to keep themselves fresh, robust and progressing, fighting the ever-present threat of obsolescence.

Also included under this mission-critical category of ethos is the legal and corporate history of the organisation, along with its reputation.

Today, with the world facing major crises ranging from climate change and environmental degradation to energy supply and demand issues, the ethos of a company needs to be environmentally and socially friendly.[262]

Ethos is not a nicety for a company, it's a necessity for survival. Business guru Arie de Geus in *The Living Company* highlights cohesion and identity as essential to a company's ability to build a community and a 'persona' for itself, upon which a strong, living brand may be based.

Ethos is key to survival and success. Michael Porter has argued that no organisation can be successful unless it has something unique to offer to the world and that good strategy can only be based on being different from everybody else. It's in the ethos that an organisation defines what makes it different and unique. Peter Schwartz, Chairman of the Global Business Network (GBN), has warned that we have to be both different and better than the next guy to succeed in the long run.

The next most important dimension of organisational systems after their ethos is the people running them. Enron was brought down primarily by unethical practices of its directors. In this category, it's important to consider such factors as: the quality, integrity and productivity of staff, staff retention rates (high staff turnover is a symptom of failing governance), as well as how motivated and incentivised staff are, how inspired they are as parts of a whole system.

Then we need to assess the assets of the organisation. Are its products and services effective and relevant? How strong is its knowledge base? How valuable is the company's PR and media profile, as well as its online profile? Are its corporate documents, trademarks and intellectual property in order? What is that copyrighted intellectual material worth?

In addition to having a robust, living ethos, productive and energised staff and valuable assets, any organisation needs financial stability and growth to achieve its purposes. Is there fiscal discipline and health in the company? Does it have both well-established and new revenue streams? Are the auditors happy? Are the stakeholders and shareholders happy with a consistent financial performance?

The system of the organisation requires many sub-systems to work well. How efficient and effective are its technology systems? What about its management systems? And its knowledge management and competitor intelligence systems? De Geus sees sensitivity to the environment as a key part of a company's ability to learn and adapt. Does the company have a responsive system for receiving and processing customer feedback? How pleasing to customers is its interface with them? Finally, does the company have vigorous, well-managed risk management in place?

The last factor to take into account in assessing whether the organisation system is future-facing and pointing in the right direction is the stability and vitality of its networks, including customer relations and loyalty, stakeholder relations (including employees, partners, suppliers, etc.), its shareholder relations and how it fits into its regulatory framework (i.e. does it have alignment with regulators and the general public they represent?). Another important factor in networking is how competitive the organisation is (its performance benchmarked against that of its competitors).

Taking all these factors into account, plotting them on the FutureFinder system, will show an organisation whether it's got what it takes to find its optimal future.

The alternative is retrogression: the road to oblivion.

13
Finding the future for nations

'Those who make peaceful revolution impossible
will make violent revolution inevitable.'
President John F. Kennedy, *Address on the First
Anniversary of the Alliance for Progress*
(13 March 1962)

There are 193 member states of the United Nations (www.
un.org), a huge increase on the 51 countries which founded
the international body after the Second World War.

Each of these nations has a common future for its populations.
There are principles of social, economic and political
development. In 'The Future We Want', adopted at Rio de
Janeiro, Brazil, in June 2012, the UN declared: 'The UN is
working with governments, civil society and other partners
to shape an ambitious sustainable development framework to
meet the needs of both people and planet, providing economic
transformation and opportunity to lift people out of poverty,
advancing social justice and protecting the environment.'[263]

Since the UN was established there has been no Third World
War, so it must be doing something right. Nonetheless, there've
been dozens of regional wars and the world came close to a

nuclear holocaust during the Cuban missile crisis in October 1962. And there was always the Cold War, with its M.A.D. doctrine – deterrence through Mutual Assured Destruction – to keep nerves on edge until the fall of communism in 1989.

But we cannot rely on the United Nations alone to guarantee there won't be a Third World War in this century. I'll argue, rather, that nations need to move beyond the bounds of ideology if they wish to progress under twenty-first-century operating conditions – and to avoid a new global conflict of unimaginable proportions.

It's time for governments to get scientific about the future of the nation they're elected to lead.

Among other things, that means we must accept that it's not ideology that can unite a nation, provide peace and propel its people towards progress. On the contrary, ideology has been the major abject failure of modern politics. It's by far the most divisive force on the planet.

In my address 'The Compelling Benefits of a Scientific Approach to South Africa's Future' delivered at a book launch in Sandton, South Africa on 17 July 2013, I showed that social ideology has not, and cannot, provide the governing principles to guide the destiny of any nation. In science, rather, lies the best hope for our common future.

That ideology has caused mayhem on Earth for centuries can hardly be denied. It took the USA into Vietnam and South Africa to the brink of bloody civil war through its systems of apartheid. Think, too, of the religious wars in Europe after the Reformation. Reflect on the colossal twentieth-century battles fought in the name of capitalism, communism and fascism.

The leading cause of death in the world today is not cancer, it's ideology. We can quantify that statement with an illustration from history. In my talk that night, I calculated the rate of deaths caused by the main ideological struggles of the previous century:

> Just before 11 a.m. on Sunday, 28 June 1914, near Sarajevo's Latin Bridge, a 24-year-old Serbian radical called Gustavo Princip fired two shots which assassinated Archduke Franz Ferdinand and his wife Sophie. This terrorist act triggered

a complex chain reaction of political events. As heir to the Austro-Hungarian throne, the archduke's death could not go unanswered. In response, this empire soon declared war on Serbia. But allies of both sides reacted and became embroiled in the conflict which escalated into the First World War. Then in 1918, the peace of Versailles ended this war – but has been widely seen as one of the causes of the Second World War due to the severe conditions it imposed on the defeated Germany. After the Second World War, the two new superpowers emerging from that international conflict, the USA and the USSR, entered into a Cold War between communism and capitalism which lasted until the fall of the Berlin Wall in 1989.

So between 28 June 1914 and 9 November 1989, when the guards at the checkpoints of East Berlin first allowed East Germans to freely pass into West Berlin, there had been two world wars, followed by a Cold War from 1947, all triggered in a chain reaction by two bullets from one young assassin.

I then totted up the military and civilian deaths in this tragic chain reaction as displayed in Table 3.

War	Ideological conflict	Estimated lives lost
First World War	Serbian independence from Austro-Hungarian empire	17 million
Second World War	Nazi and Italian fascism versus Western democracy and Russian communism	60 million
Cold War	Vietnam War/Second Indochina War (1955–75)	2 million
	Korean War (1950–53)	1.2 million
	Soviet War in Afghanistan (1979–89)	1.5 million
	Total lives lost between 28 June 1914 and 9 November 1989	81.7 million
	Rate of lives lost in political conflict between 1914–89	= over 1 million deaths per year = 2,740 deaths per day

Table 3: Lives lost in ideological conflict in a chain reaction of interconnected twentieth-century conflict

Table 3, showing a rate of a million deaths per year, or 2,740 deaths per day, in political conflicts during that 1914–89 period, illustrates the failure of ideological governance of nation states and their alliances. We're talking about the most catastrophic political chain reaction of all time, triggered by Princip's two bullets fired in a misguided rage. Ideology, it seems, is deadly. Yet political systems and parties today are still largely formed around ideological principles.

This adherence to ideology for ordering societies no longer makes any sense. Given the scale of challenges facing nations in our time, from climate change to the energy crisis, continuing along the same path to governance of nations would be suicidal.

I propose a switch to science as a framework of governance for twenty-first-century societies. Consider, instead, the seven benefits of adopting a scientific approach to addressing problems of a common reality shared by population groups. Science, it turns out, is the key to innovation, to understanding the laws of nature, to problem solving, and even to wealth creation through technological innovation and best practice.

In short, taking these seven benefits together in Table 4, we can see science as a peaceful, knowledge-based, rational, innovative, problem-solving, environmentally-friendly, future-facing approach to the development of societies beset by deep-rooted global issues.

In addition, I've developed a practical future monitoring system to assist nations in finding the path to their optimal future. It's called FutureFinder for nations. Like FutureFinder for individuals and organisations, it rates thirty future factors which, together, determine and cause the future.

Nations, like organisations, should aim for their optimum, which is their most favourable state. In biology, the optimum is the most advantageous condition for growth and reproduction. It's up to the nation's leaders to give voice to, and articulate, their unique optimum. What FutureFinder does is to evaluate as objectively as possible thirty future factors which can take a country towards its maximum destiny.

As for organisations in the previous chapter, it's the ethos that lies at a nation's heart, along with the various roles played by its people. In this all-important category of ethos are included such issues as male–female relations and rights; the role, dynamism and justice of its constitution; the rule of law in the society; its levels of democracy, freedom and independence; its historical record of evolution as a civilisation; the structured social balance between government, the private sector and civil society; the integrity of its leaders in government and business (as measured by such indices as corruption and transparency measurements), and the degree of embedded violence in the history and institutions of the land.

How can a society be happy if there isn't a just balance and equality between male and female, between mothers and fathers, brothers and sisters? How can peoples be free unless there are constitutional protections and the rule of law for all? How can politics and the economy work properly in a climate of corruption? How can there be peace if there are structural and institutional forms of violence? How can the future be promising for a whole nation if it hasn't shown any signs of evolving towards an increasing level of civilisation in its history?

Just as important as the ethos and governance of a society are its people.

In this dimension, FutureFinder looks at such elements as family structures and the nation's general demographic profile. What is the nation's fertility rate per woman, and the nation's age structure? What is the ratio between its working age group – people between, say, fifteen and sixty – and its older population sector? What is the general health standard and life expectancy of the people?

Most importantly, the system asks how stable the nation's family structure (marriage and divorce rate) is, since it's vital to a nation's future to keep creating people and human capital for labour, productivity and growth. Since the cities and towns are where wealth can be produced on a mass scale for larger population groups, there also has to be a high level of urbanisation in the nation.

It's one thing to have a positive demographic profile, including fertility rate and age profile as well as stable social structures, but without a fine education system the nation will not optimise its human resources. So FutureFinder evaluates such factors as literacy levels, the competitiveness of its education system and the knowledge base held by its universities and colleges.

Characteristic of science	Benefit to society
1. Science provides an ideology-neutral framework for addressing issues and problems. It promotes reason and freedom of thought.	Being ideology-neutral, as well as gender-blind and colour-blind, science can advance social order and peace. It's the ideal framework for discussing and solving common social problems.
2. Science provides a code of ethics, enshrining the values of discipline, professionalism and precision of thinking, as well as the benefits of cooperative thinking.	The disciplines of science enable societies and people to get things done with a high degree of professionalism and integrity.
3. Science has proven itself to be the best way to gain and apply knowledge.	Science can create a knowledge-based society.
4. Science encourages innovation and problem solving due to the fact that science is essentially knowledge which is based on the laws of nature, that is: how things really work, not how we think they will work.	Science promotes technological innovation. It's a model for steering our evolution as a society towards continuous improvement.
5. Science will teach us how to be more environmentally friendly.	The long-range social future will be dominated by the environment, and science is the best way we know for harnessing knowledge of nature.
6. Science will give us greater confidence about ourselves.	The problem-solving capacity of science, under an umbrella of rational peaceful pursuit of solutions and knowledge, will boost human confidence.
7. Science can increase our capacity to predict by building detailed and accurate models for regular behaviours.	With its predictive capacity, science can foster proactive thinking and improve the evolutionary skill of anticipation.

Table 4: The seven benefits of science to society

We are creatures of society and nature and the two worlds are interconnected in the cosmic Biomatrix of systems. So we should not divorce ourselves from nature – what we call these days the environment. Here, FutureFinder looks at such questions as what the country's natural resources are, including mineral deposits and agricultural fertility and productivity. How degraded are its major ecosystems? How will climate change affect weather, agriculture and lifestyle in the country? How geographically central is the nation in terms of international access and proximity not just to markets but also to important resources? How big a problem is air, water and soil pollution? The nation's future is inseparable from its environment: the two are one.

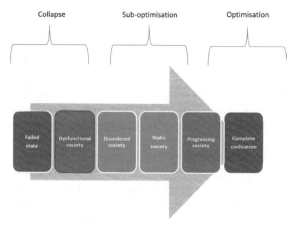

Figure 34: Finding the future direction for nations

The next key dimension considered in FutureFinder for nations is the question of the energy resources it has to power up its economy and households, fuelling production and consumption. We're talking about energy security and self-sufficiency, as measured by how much fuel has to be imported as opposed to developed within its own boundaries. Today, that means the three big fuels of oil, coal and gas in addition to nuclear and renewable sources of electricity.

It's important to evaluate not just the energy resources, but the governance, stability and infrastructure for managing and distributing energy produced and imported. For example,

Nigeria is rich in both oil and conflict. The left hand takes away what the right hand produces.

Energy drives all systems and all economies. So a country's future wealth, productivity and progress depends directly on both its endowment and governance of energy resources. It's important to gauge pricing of energy, too. Skyrocketing costs of electricity and fuel will impair economic growth and push up the cost of living.

Of course, there are several other factors on top of the energy system which enable economic productivity and wealth creation. We measure GDP and the size of the economy in question only as a starting point. The next aspect to diagnose is the fiscal health of the country's public finances. How much debt has the government taken on compared to its GDP? What is the trade balance between imports and exports? Is state and municipal expenditure in keeping with budgetary targets and local tax bases?

To keep an economy robust, it needs to be productive and competitive, while encouraging innovation and entrepreneurship. Is the creative economy growing in size year on year? Is there sufficient investment in R&D? Are there free-market mechanisms in place to allow supply and demand to function according to the laws of the market? Is there good corporate governance in the business sector? Is there commitment in business to the good of society and the environment as our shared reality? In the end, though, the proof of the pudding is in the eating, and we need to look at the real living standards and cost of living as experienced by the population in their daily lives.

It's hard work to build a strong future for a society. FutureFinder evaluates thirty factors which, together, produce the common future of nations.

Isn't it worth turning to a science of the future to guide nations to their destiny? Ideology doesn't work as a governing ethos for national systems. It cannot unite diverse population groups. It cannot solve technical and physical problems. It cannot save the environment.

Science is the hope of nations in this century.

14

Progression

'But the real and legitimate goal of the sciences is the endowment of human life with new inventions and riches.'

Francis Bacon, *Novum Organum* (1620)

'Unsustainable trends end.'

Phillip Longman, *The Empty Cradle* (2004)

If science is the hope of nations, how can its methods and knowledge best be applied to ensure hope turns to vision, and vision, in turn, becomes a mission which can be planned and implemented in reality?

One pioneer of the scientific method, Francis Bacon, was under no illusions as to the power of science, not just as an academic discipline but as a tool of social and economic progress. In 1620, before the Industrial Revolution, he predicted the rise of a vast mass of inventions.[264]

Actually, I prefer the word 'progression' as the target of all our endeavours, partly because the word 'progress' has run its course and is probably exhausted of meaning due to its long history in which controversial events and policies, including colonialism and the doomed conflict between communism and capitalism, have been advanced in its name. Whereas 'progress' is a heady, disputed and emotive word, 'progression' seems to be more neutral in tone, implying gradual development towards a more advanced, and optimal, state. Both words are derived from the Latin root *progressus*, meaning an advance forward. The other advantage of the alternative term 'progression' is that it speaks to the action, or movement, towards something better as a continuous event, whereas 'progress' seems to be the end in itself. Rather than aiming for progress, we could aim to be in a permanent state of progression.

This concept is more in keeping with the ideology-neutral stance of science. It's realistic rather than idealistic. And, it's consistent with the physics of time, which sees time as having one direction only – forwards.

Progression may be defined simply as advancing in a forward direction in space and time. To advance in space means to improve the physical world. To advance in time is to invest in a stronger future. Ultimately, progression can do both.

Progression involves building goodness on all levels.

The FutureFinder system, introduced in the previous three chapters, is one method for monitoring progression. Instead of a vague commitment to progress, there is a knowledge-based, periodically monitored system promoting ongoing progression. What gets measured, gets treasured.

The good news is that the relationship between knowledge and development is self-reinforcing. New technologies and wealth produced by applying knowledge feed the production of yet more new knowledge. This virtuous circle is the essence of progression.

The model in Figure 35 has been effectively used for hundreds of years of social development ever since Bacon's 1620 forecast of a new future filled with a mass of inventions. Applying scientific knowledge leads to better technologies and systems which, in turn, unearth more facts about the world.

Accompanying this approach is a new, proactive attitude to the future, stripped of the moods and emotions clouding both pessimism and optimism. Laplace spoke about the mathematics of hope. This renowned mathematician and thinker believed that various illusions and delusions tend to feed subjective forms of hope, which should be replaced by logical decision making, more in keeping with the scientific viewpoint, which states, in the Copernican principle, that we always occupy non-special positions in the grand scheme of things: 'The opinion that man has long been placed in the centre of the universe, considering himself the special object of the cares of nature, leads each individual to make himself the centre of a more or less extended sphere and to believe that hazard has preference for him. Sustained by this belief, players often risk considerable sums at games when they know that the chances are unfavourable. In the conduct of life a similar opinion may sometimes have advantages; but most often it leads to disastrous enterprises. Here, as everywhere, illusions are dangerous and truth alone is generally useful.'[265]

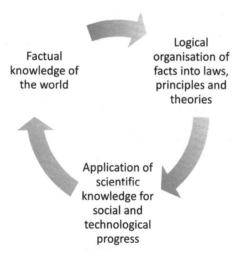

Figure 35: Virtuous circle of knowledge and development

Even when things aren't certain, we can still use probability reasoning to spread risks, to weigh up options and to choose the most favourable courses of action. It's about aligning ourselves and our systems with positive evolutionary development, to find the most advantageous positions and states, pointing each system in the direction of progression.

The added dimension of dynamic time analysis, the fourth dimension of Einstein's space–time, will enhance our current predominantly spatial understanding of the world. By unlocking the inner workings of the whole of space–time, not just the operations of our three-dimensional world of space, we'll usher in the greatest scientific show on Earth, filled with Bacon's vast mass of inventions.

In my view, as a futurist, we're destined to evolve into highly advanced time-literate beings.

Each human being is already a simple time machine. We have a rear view mirror called memory and we have a windscreen called foresight to look at the road ahead. As little time machines, humans are moving rapidly into the future whether we're ready or not.

Time, even more than money, makes the world go round. Everything, including our lives, passes through cycles determined by the laws of nature and the laws of social development. Most of life is predictable because most of life is caused within these predetermined cycles of existence. In some ways, this is reassuring since it takes away the existential angst of being responsible for the whole of our lives, of being abandoned in the state Jean-Paul Sartre once described as being condemned to be free.

Humans are creatures of time, just as much as they belong to the three dimensional world of space. Like time itself, we have to be future-facing. We can learn to preconstruct the future as its causal influences weave together the complex tapestry of the future.

We can become incredibly dynamic through adding understanding of time in order to make us 4D beings. The philosopher David Hume was correct when he said: 'We advance, rather than retard our existence; and following what seems the natural succession of time, proceed from past to present, and from present to future. By which means we conceive the future as flowing every moment nearer us, and the past as retiring … we consider the one [the future] as continually increasing, and the other [the past] as continually diminishing.'[266]

Yes, the future is increasing and the past diminishing as we speak. Face forward, where life is increasing, not backwards, where life is diminishing. Advance. We've tried progress. Now let's try progression. It's the permanent condition of moving forwards, of gradually building up goodness in the world.

15

Prologue for our century

'The frivolity and boredom which unsettle the established order, the vague foreboding of something unknown, these are the heralds of approaching change.'

G.W.F. Hegel, *Phenomenology of Spirit* (1807)

The defining choices humanity makes about what kind of society is best could well become irreversible in this century, due to the limited amount of time left to solve a growing list of potentially terminal problems.

Now, more than ever, it's imperative to make wise decisions about a range of issues facing us, from the future of the family to sustainable industrial energy systems, from environmental stewardship to whether to begin a new human colony on Mars, from creating viable social and economic systems to preventing a Third World War. The stakes are high. Implicated in these upcoming decisions will be our whole endeavour to establish a lasting and beautiful civilisation on earth. Further down the road, the long-term survival of our species will be threatened by human depopulation and global ageing.

Many of the issues which demand public attention in the coming decades will arise as part of four revolutionary changes facing us in these times, outlined in Table 5 below: (1) a revolution in the demography of the world, which, in turn, will drive (2) a gradual global shift in power; (3) an environmental revolution, and (4) an energy revolution. How we respond to these four changes of order will determine whether or not global society faces an epic fall (see 'low road' outcomes below) or an ascent to a higher level of civilisation (see 'high road' outcomes below).

Sometimes I wonder how it can be possible that the modern world, with all its technology, knowledge and science, could have ended up as it is now – on such a tragic precipice where the scale of challenges has the potential to derail global society.

Type of revolution	Nature of challenge	'Low road' outcome	'High road' outcome
Demographic revolution	Human depopulation and global ageing	Humans become an endangered species	Family-friendly civilisation evolves
Global revolution	Shifts in balance of international power	Third World War	New alliance of civilisations spearheaded by UN
Environmental revolution	Climate change and degradation of the environment	Nature becomes increasingly inhospitable to humans	New pact with nature as part of quest for social harmony
Energy revolution	Decline of fossil fuels as the source of choice for industrial power	Resource wars and energy price riots	Sustainable energy systems

Table 5: Four changes of order in the twenty-first century

A revolution arises from a critical challenge which drives the forces of change. The goal of revolution is to bring about the overthrow of a perceived unsustainable order. What is unquestionable from viewing Table 5 is that we live in watershed times, pregnant with dangers on an unprecedented scale. Each of the four revolutions outlined in the Table could go south – with fearful consequences.

The first change of order that's already underway is demographic. The major issue of the century ahead may be described as an invisible catastrophe unfolding in ultra-slow motion: human depopulation.

Most advanced nations have disastrously low birth rates, with mass-scale abortion on demand killing forty million babies every year in the world. These ageing nations do not replace the numbers of their dying with equivalent numbers of the newly born. Consequently, they're increasingly dependent on immigrant populations to keep up the required numbers of people in the working-age group, of fifteen to fifty-nine, relative to old, state-dependent people.

In addition, institutions like marriage, which nurture human procreation and the development of children, are under threat. Fortunately, humanity has a timeless self-preservation lifecycle which goes something like this:

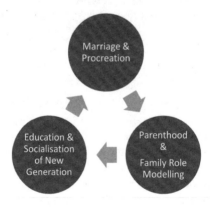

Figure 36: The human perpetuation cycle

The preservation of the human race, and the perpetuation of nations, depends on this simple cycle of procreation and family modelling. Marriage and family life are the keys to the human cycle of life. But various practices and values are threatening this cycle in Figure 36.

For example, there is mass abortion on demand which is contributing to the decrease in birth rates. Since the US Supreme Court ruled, on 22 January 1973, that a woman's right to an abortion was protected by the country's constitution, the yearly abortion rate in the country has now reached 1.5 million. Even home abortions are becoming popular, including in Britain, creating a culture in which women can terminate their babies in the comfort of their own homes. The British Pregnancy Advisory Service (bpas)[267] proudly announced that a record 10,000 women had an abortion at home in 2005, using the abortion pill, making up a third of the 32,000 terminations it provided in that year.[268] The pill, also known as EMA – or early medical abortion – has been criticised by pro-life campaigners as encouraging a 'DIY' culture for ending pregnancies.

Practising abortion and dispensing birth-control pills, both on a mass scale, will cause a nose-dive in any society's birth rate. The contraceptive pill was first licensed in 1960. Within ten years, 43 per cent of married women in America were 'on the pill'. The rapid take-up of the birth-control pill throughout the West after it was licensed in the 1960s, and the spread of a culture of 'abortion on demand' after the practice was legalised in the United States in the 1970s, illustrate how quickly mass societies can disseminate new cultural messages and social practices across their extensive infrastructures.

Birth rates in most developed countries have fallen so far that they are now well below population replacement levels. That means more people die than are born in these nations. That may not sound serious, but in the long run it means these population groups have peaked and are headed for biological decline. Collapsing birth rates have become the norm in highly developed countries from Italy to Denmark, from Germany to Belgium. Of the twenty nations with the lowest birth rates in the world, eighteen are in Europe.[269]

European nations with falling birth rates are rapidly becoming ageing societies. If Europe's fertility rate does not rise, by 2050 the median age of a European will be fifty.[270]

Take Germany. Formerly one of the most powerful nations on Earth, its birth rate has stood for ten years at 1.3 children per woman, below the replacement rate of 2.1. By 2050, a third of Germany's population is likely to be over sixty-five and Germans will be among the oldest people on earth. Without population growth, Nietzsche's *Übermensch* turns inexorably into the *alte Menschen*. The superman becomes the old man.

As populations age like this, so the size of the working population shrinks relative to the total population. More and more elderly people need to be financially provided for by fewer and fewer economically active citizens: 'At the moment, the elderly make up 16 percent of the EU population; within five years, they will make up 27 percent… The current median age of 37.7 years will rise to 52.3 by 2050, and the working-age population will fall to 50 percent of the total.'[271]

Marriage, too, is being crippled. Yet you don't get any institution anywhere in the world more fundamental than marriage. Our family dissolution rates are alarming. Marriage was designed from the beginning of time to protect the family, and, through it, childhood and parenting. Now its long-term survival is under threat from two principal sources: increased divorce rates and the practice of cohabitation.

Statistics show that divorce is a very familiar trauma in advanced nations. We're becoming 'Generation Ex'. Recent divorce rates in European and North American countries show that a high percentage of marriages end in divorce:[272]

Just about every second marriage in these countries in Table 6 ends up on the rocks.

The average length of marriages in the United Kingdom has fallen to 11.5 years. The UK's Office for National Statistics (ONS) reported on 31 August 2005 that the country's divorce rate had reached its highest levels since 1996 and had risen for the fourth successive year. [273] Divorce on this scale feeds into other social problems:

- Children of divorced parents are statistically more likely themselves to go through a divorce.[274]

- Divorced people are much more likely to commit suicide than married individuals.[275]

- The emotional trauma of separation is typically compounded by financial difficulties arising from divorce: in the year 2000, 45 per cent of divorced women in the USA suffered a drop in their standard of living following their divorces.[276]

Russia	65%
Sweden	64%
Ukraine	63%
Belgium	56%
Finland	56%
United Kingdom	53%
United States	49%
Canada	45%
France	43%
Germany	41%
Netherlands	41%
Switzerland	40%

Table 6: Percentages of marriages ending in divorce in major Western countries

Regarding the growing popularity of 'living together', Civitas,[277] the Institute for the Study of Civil Society in Britain, points out that while only 5 per cent of single women lived with a man before getting married in the UK in the mid-1960s, by the 1990s this figure had escalated to 70 per cent. An increase from 5 per cent to 70 per cent within three decades indicates that a fundamental cultural shift took place in regard to marriage in that country.[278]

The age of cohabitation has arrived in the West.[279] Not only are couples opting in huge numbers for cohabitation, lowering the marriage rate in Western societies, but more and more urbanites are staying single for much longer. Both trends impact on birth rates, marriage and the future of the family in urban societies.

A similar paradigm shift towards increased cohabitation has occurred in Europe. Civitas has researched the merits of marriage versus cohabitation. They conclude that cohabiting is less likely than marriage to lead to a long-term stable commitment.[280] About 15 per cent of one-parent families are created by the break-up of cohabiting unions. Over 20 per cent of UK children are born to cohabiting couples.

Another symptom of family disorder is the rise of violence in homes. Violence against children and women is out of control in our societies. Domestic violence now accounts for a quarter of all murders in Britain.[281] The UK charity Refuge (www.refuge. org.uk) has called for a national domestic violence strategy. Refuge shares the following facts about this kind of violence in the UK:

- One in four women is abused during her lifetime.

- One in nine is severely physically abused each year.

- Two women are killed each week.[282]

Domestic violence[283] is rarely a one-off – incidents generally become more frequent and severe over time. Other indicators of growing violence in our homes include:

- In Russia, over 12,000 women die every year at their partners' hands.[284]

A 2002 survey by the Women's Council of Moscow State University indicated that up to 18 per cent of Russian women suffer 'regular and cruel physical treatment' at the hands of a husband or lover while 96,000 abused women turned to the Russian Association of Crisis Centers for Women for help in 2002.

- In 2000, 1,247 women in the USA were killed by an intimate partner while there were 691,710 non-fatal incidents of violence committed by current or former spouses/ partners in 2001.

- In 1999, intimate partner murders accounted for 32 per cent of the murders of females and 4 per cent of the murders of males in the USA.

- According to the second survey of women's status carried out by the All China Women's Federation, domestic violence in China affects around 30 per cent of women, although these figures are only the tip of the iceberg.

- A UN survey of violence against children published in August 2006 found that up to 275 million young people worldwide endure physical, sexual and psychological attacks.

- An estimated one million children in the UK suffer domestic violence.

On 6 January 2006, US President Bush signed the Violence Against Women Act, H.R. 3402, following what the National Coalition Against Domestic Violence call an epidemic of intimate partner violence and abuse in the nation. The coalition's figures are that one in four women will experience this form of violence during her lifetime.

Household violence is expensive as well as dangerous for women and children. The National Coalition Against Domestic Violence estimates that the total annual direct and indirect costs of intimate partner violence in the USA is $67 billion for health care and ambulance service expenses, lost productivity, damage to property, costs of the criminal justice process, etc., with the costs to employers somewhere between $3 and $13 billion each year.[285]

It is not just the nature of society that gets changed by these demographic shifts. On the political stage, demography also determines destiny.

In particular, falling birth rates, leading eventually to depopulation, herald future shifts in political and economic influence. That's because a nation's population size and population age profile help to determine its economic composition, size and clout.

Today's rising demographic stars could become tomorrow's new international powers. In particular, depopulation and global ageing will lead to the global decline of many Western powers, especially nations which are not self-sufficient in energy resources.

In Chapter 8, we saw that humanity's total population size could start to decrease in absolute terms before the middle of the century, with global fertility rates, already half of what they were in 1972, set to sink further. It was revealed that sixty-two countries, making up almost half the world's population, now have fertility rates at, or below, the replacement rate of 2.1, including most of the industrial world and Asian powers like China, Taiwan and South Korea.

Some nations, too, have literally started to shrink, including important economic powers such as Japan and Russia. In most areas of the world, families, the factories of human capital to supply future labour forces, are shrinking in size. In the long run, the depopulation bomb will threaten the survival of the nation state as the main unit of political organisation.

Chapter 8 also discussed global population ageing, with dozens of societies in Asia, Europe and in the Americas turning grey. Since old people need and spend less than younger population groups, this lowers demand, slowing down supply and therefore production. In addition, more and more people require support in terms of medical care and pensions, with a tax base fed by fewer and fewer workers. This is why demographic cycles tend to underpin many economic and social cycles (see, for example, Figures 17 and 18). We concluded that if family size shrinks, the nation eventually shrinks, along with its labour force, its tax base and, finally, its wealth.

Benjamin Franklin was optimistic about the future of America because he knew his young nation's birth rate was double that of Europe at the time. It's countries in the Middle East and in Africa now which have the world's highest birth rates, not America – nor any Western nation, for that matter.

In my view, the demographic revolution we've been discussing will result in the following ten major shifts in global power in the twenty-first century in terms of winners and losers as measured by political and economic influence:

Nation/continent/power	Forecast	Forecast period	Reason(s)
1. India	WINNER Rising to become Asia's America, ultimately surpassing China in size and influence	2040–2100	Youthful population with strong birth rate in a free-market democracy and a rapidly growing economy
2. Africa	WINNER Rise of advanced nations within Africa and increased global influence of the continent	2040–2100	World's most youthful populations; increased intra-Africa unity and trade; impact of scientific knowledge still to be felt
3. UK & Europe	LOSER Gradual economic decline; followed by religiously and racially inspired social unrest	2030–2100	Demographic decline; increased dependence on immigrant populations; unravelling of social cohesion and culture
4. Russia	WINNER, THEN LOSER Golden period; followed by decline and increasing social unrest	Up to about 2030–2050; second half of century	Depopulation
5. Japan	LOSER Gradual economic and social decline	Throughout century	Depopulation
6. USA	WINNER, THEN LOSER Continued supremacy; followed by gradual decline	Up to about 2055; second half of century	Demographic decline and ageing, along with overextended resources and spending

7. China	WINNER, THEN LOSER Increasing social disorder; short-lived position as world's number one economy followed by decline; reinvention as a great and free Chinese civilisation	Up to mid-century; 2030–2040; throughout second half of century; from about 2050 onwards	Demographic gender imbalance and ageing, depopulation after mid-century, as well as political implosion of one-party state
8. Faith-based societies (i.e. which nurture religion)	WINNER Rising political and economic influence; eventually surpassing influence of secular societies (ones undermining religion and the human family), especially through regional, national and global alliances	2030–2100	Pro-natal policies and values will see faith-rich population groups maintain higher-than replacement fertility rates to maintain demographic vigour in a world facing the depopulation bomb
9. The nation state	LOSER Decline in relation to new local, regional and global powers and alliances	Throughout the century but intensifying in the second half of century	Demographic decline and realignment according to civilisational, family and gender values
10. Mixed economy models	WINNER A shift towards 'eco-nomics' in which business works together with the state and NGOs to create and maintain sustainable economic models which benefit society and protect the environment	2020–2100	Crises of energy, environment and economics will, together, drive change in how we do economics and how we make wealth; the new emerging powers will embrace mixed pragmatic economy models rather than 'pure' capitalism or 'pure' socialism as the bankruptcy of ideology as a governing ethos is confirmed and as the West declines in influence

Table 7: Ten demographic winners and losers of the twenty-first century

In short, the depopulation bomb will explode in this century. By the time the dust settles on this crisis, the world will be a different place. Secularism will be on its deathbed because it cannot perpetuate the human species or maintain the demographic vigour of its population groups; faith-based societies will be in the ascendancy. The nation state itself will be in advanced stages of decline. In its place, local, regional, national and international alliances based on values, including preservation of the human family, will be dominant. The United Nations will become increasingly important to governance of global human society. Economics will have evolved into 'eco-nomics' and mixed economic models will be adopted by most civilisations and societies.

Africa in the second half of the century may wield the kind of influence Europe has today, while Europe itself will be a pale shadow of its former glory, riven by ethnic conflict and social tensions accompanying economic decline. China, too, will be undergoing a painful transition to political freedom. The *Pax Americana* will peak by about mid-century. By then, India will be on its way to becoming the most influential economy and society in the world but in a time in which nation states won't matter as much as they've done throughout the Modern Age.

The third change of order we face this century, following the demographic revolution and its accompanying global power shifts, is environmental.

Leading scientists assessing the dangers posed to civilisation have kept the famous Doomsday Clock[286] at five minutes to midnight from 2012 in recognition of their belief that climate change has become one of the greatest threats to humankind. In fact, the Doomsday scientists regard global warming as a peril equal to that posed by the possibility of mass nuclear destruction. Humanity, they believe, is at its most critical crossroads in generations.

The biggest concern about climate change, in my view, is that an a-synergia is developing between nature and civilisation which, left unchecked, would render Earth largely uninhabitable for advanced industrial societies.

Humanity needs to protect land, sea and air making up its habitat. As Ernst Friederich Schumacher, author of the little

1973 classic of economics, *Small is Beautiful*, wrote: 'Among material resources, the greatest, unquestionably, is the land. Study how a society uses its land, and you can come to pretty reliable conclusions as to what its future will be.'

Pollution and overexploitation, we know, have degraded the planet and the fragile splendour of its many and varied ecosystems. Ultimately, economic systems develop from underlying ecosystems supplying food, water and power.

Humankind has just entered a disturbing epoch of planetary instability as Table 8 indicates (p. 156). Atmospheric and environmental degradation have each reached a critical stage. Seven billion tons of carbon are added to our atmosphere annually by industrial society. This could double to fourteen billion if current rates of industrial production and development continue. Extreme weather arising from the Earth's atmospheric imbalances is inflicting widespread destruction on societies across the globe each year, emptying state coffers of much-needed funds.

Plainly and simply put, an escalation in the rate of disasters and extreme weather events shows deterioration in the stability of the environment and atmosphere in which we live. There are many human inputs which are causal factors in this decline. We should not rip apart the ecological tent in which humanity exists.

Planetary disorder will increase economic challenges through two main factors. First, the costs of dealing with global warming, pollution and environmental degradation will drain public coffers of both rich and developing nations. Second, food and water security are being threatened by environmental depletion and ruination.

A combination of climate change and environmental depletion can topple a society over into extinction. When environments near their exhaustion point, there may be a mass exodus of economic migrants looking for a new environmental home, or heightened death rates through killings arising from infighting over scarce resources, starvation and disease. Either way, society breaks down.

Nature of problem	Examples	Causes	Consequences
Increased rate of natural disasters: the rise of a 'disaster a day' world.[287]	In 2006, there were 427 reported natural disasters that killed more than 23,000 people, affected almost 143 million others, and were the cause of more than US$34.5 billion in economic damages.[288]	Pollution; global warming; natural events.	Loss of life, economic damages, increase in refugees.
Climate change.	Changes in rainfall and weather patterns; unnatural warming of the Earth's atmosphere (greenhouse effect); rising sea surface temperatures; increased water vapour/precipitation in air.	Increased levels of heat-trapping carbon dioxide, from the burning of fossil fuels, car engines, furnaces, combustion units for generation of electricity, are poisoning the atmosphere.	Less stable atmosphere. Increased intensity of tropical storms and thunderstorms feeding off warm wet air. Increases in extreme weather events: hurricanes, tornadoes, floods, heatwaves, earthquakes, tsunamis. Melting ice caps and rising sea levels. Crowded river deltas in southern Asia and Egypt, along with small Asian island nations are most at risk from rise in sea level. Increased spread of diseases like malaria and pneumonia.

Environmental depletion and degradation.	Soil erosion, desertification, salination of land.	Deforestation, mismanagement of agriculture, overexploitation of land and marine fisheries.	Drought and water shortages, increased risk of flooding, lower agricultural output, famine, destruction of certain habitats, threatened extinction of many species of animals and plants, loss of biodiversity.
Pollution.	Polluted air and rivers, and more acidic seas. Ozone depletion. Acid rain. Arsenic in groundwater.	Pesticides, carbon emissions, combustion of fossil fuels. Chlorofluorocarbons (CFCs) decompose ozone atoms. CFCs, halons and hydrochlorofluorocarbons (HCFCs) contribute to both ozone depletion and climate change. Oceans have already absorbed a third of the world's emissions of carbon dioxide.	Poor air quality, health risks, lower agricultural and marine yields. Increased toxins in the environment. Threat to microorganisms and the food chain. Rising levels of acid in the sea threaten fish stocks and the marine food chain. One quarter of the world's population is exposed to unhealthy concentrations of air pollutants. More than a billion people, a sixth of the world's population, do not have access to clean drinking water. Contaminated water, especially by arsenic, has put the health of about 50 million people at risk in Asia alone. Long-term exposure to arsenic via drinking water causes cancer of the skin, lungs, bladder and kidneys.

Table 8: Four kinds of planetary disorder

Civilisation harnesses resources to make human society as safe and meaningful as possible. Underlying the economy and society are ecosystems providing the resources and energy for both human life and industrial production: water and wheat, fruit and fish, oil and ore, gold and gas, stone and steel, rice and rubber, cotton and cattle, sunlight and seed, milk and meat, vegetables and vines, and so on. Nature is the home and bedrock of civilisation, not a leafy backdrop to suburbia.

Pollution in the atmosphere and oceans is changing the Earth's planetary order and ushering in a new era of extreme weather. These days, weather records are being broken on a regular basis – the hottest year ever recorded, the worst droughts in a hundred years, the strongest storms in decades, the highest rainfall and worst floods for years, etc.

The map of the Global Drought Monitor, produced by University College London (UCL) (www.ucl.ac.uk) which measures the intensity of drought worldwide, shows a patchwork quilt of different degrees of drought affecting countries from Brazil to Indonesia, from Botswana to Iran, from Egypt to Papua New Guinea, from northern South Africa to many newly independent states of the former USSR. Drought is sweeping the USA, too. China's southwestern city of Chongqing, located along the upper reaches of the Yangtze River, has suffered its worst drought in half a century. Nearly 1.63 million people, or 5.4 per cent of the city's population, are short on drinking water.

A global audit of such marginal environments which are most at risk from climate change is urgently needed, along with international and national planning for measures to relocate population groups which will be plunged into distress when their natural environments are no longer able to carry them.

On 28 November 2005, United Nations Radio broadcast a commentary comparing global warming to weapons of mass destruction in terms of the power to cause catastrophes. Robert May, president of the Royal Society – Britain's leading scientific body – stated that the impacts of global warming are comparable to the danger posed by these fearful weapons.[289]

It's thought that by 2050, when the global population will be around nine billion, we will be using the equivalent of nearly two planets' worth of resources. Our rivers and underground water supplies have been overexploited and, in many areas, contaminated. Polluted air lowers the quality of life for millions of people in hundreds of overcrowded cities.

Out in the country, deforestation, overgrazing and intensive, mass-scale irrigation have caused widespread soil erosion, while mechanised, mono-crop, industrial farming has led to the collapse of rural communities and to depleted soil fertility. It's estimated that ten million hectares of productive land is lost every year to desertification, which now affects two-thirds of the world's agricultural land. Desertification is being blamed for forced migration and growing food insecurity among millions of people in the developing world. In the sea, we have overexploited fisheries and, far above us, the twin problems of the ozone hole and carbon dioxide build-up undermine the efficiency of the atmosphere and make climates and weather patterns more unstable.

A dangerous feedback loop is developing between degraded, eroded land and erratic, extreme weather. For example, poor quality, barren soil and deforested land cannot absorb heavy rain which flows off the ground more easily and increases the risk of flooding. The cutting down of timber on hillsides magnifies the impact of landslides. The draining of wetlands increases damage caused by flooding. And hotter average temperatures caused by global warming further dry out the thinly covered ground, as well as leading to higher degrees of water evaporation from lakes and rivers which are already under strain.

Feedback loops of this nature indicate an advanced state of deterioration. They can cause sudden, non-linear impacts which cannot be controlled.

The 2005 Millennium Ecosystem Assessment (MA), commissioned by the UN, is a landmark report on the state of the world's ecosystems. The report, drawn up by more than 1,350 scientists from 95 countries, gives a stark warning about the disastrous effects of overconsumption of natural resources on the ability of ecosystems to provide people with essential services, like food, water and fuel. The MA concluded that 60 per cent of all ecosystem services they examined are either being degraded or being used unsustainably. The ecosystem services on the brink of breakdown include fisheries, supplies of fresh water, regulation of climate and air and water purification. The MA forecasts that ecosystem degradation will worsen significantly over the next fifty years. Degradation of ecosystems on this scale increases the risks of abrupt deteriorations such as sudden loss of water quality, the creation of 'dead zones' in coastal waters, the collapse of fisheries, climate shifts and the emergence of new diseases and pests.

We cannot rule out the possibility of some socio-ecological collapses in the coming times from communities to small nations living in unsustainable environments.[290] Several communities and societies are perched precariously on crumbling ecological foundations. Costs of eco-decay are high. For example, a 700-page report on the economic impacts of global warming commissioned by the UK government in 2006 concluded that climate change could eventually shrink the global economy by as much as 20 per cent.[291]

Civilisation is housed within the environment, not the other way around. Yet it seems our civilisation has now placed itself in an increasingly conflicted relationship with nature.

Just as far-reaching and even more impactful on economies than climate change is the terminal decline of fossil fuels as the power source for industry and modern societies. Without industrial power we'll go back to the Dark Ages. The energy crisis, the fourth change of order in Table 5, may end up crippling industrial society far more effectively than even extreme weather conditions. Without cheap oil, industrial systems and cities will face energy and supply shortages, transport breakdowns, power outages and severe economic pressures.

The fourth revolution in Table 5 is the change to a new energy order beyond the domination of fossil fuels towards clean energy, including renewable and nuclear. This is the largest, most important, change to industry since the Industrial Revolution began.

In addition, our industrial economies run on non-renewable fossil fuels, especially oil. Oil and gas provide the power that runs our enormous cities and their all-important electricity grids.

But Earth's finite supplies of this energy are now quickly running out *forever*. If resources are finite it means they are limited in supply. Therefore there is a lifecycle for them with a beginning, a peak and an end.

There's increasing demand for oil and gas but decreasing supplies. Soon, world oil production will peak, and has already declined in most of the world. Oil production has fallen in sixty countries. There will be zero available oil on Earth by about 2050. Oilfields are depleting; ageing infrastructure needs upgrading and reinvestment but on high-risk terms; drilling rigs are growing old; there are no new giant oilfields being discovered; a flat world oil supply is struggling to keep up with the demand which is growing at 3 per cent annually; costs are rising and production levels are flattening.

Since oil is the primary energy source driving the global economic system, waning oil production has triggered price instability and the beginning of what is likely to be a long series of resource wars and oil terrorism focused on the oil-rich Middle East.

Long before the last drop of extractable oil has been taken out, the energy crisis will precipitate unprecedented levels of economic and political pressure on the global system. Exploding demand for oil in China and India, occurring at a time when there simply isn't going to be enough fuel to go around, will inaugurate this emergency. Diminishing supplies of oil will eventually choke off global supply chains for international trade and mass retailing, both of which are dependent on long-distance transport systems.

Mother Earth is no longer in the business of manufacturing oil; she is not going to produce more oil deposits no matter how nicely we ask her. The Oil Age, almost 150 years old now, began in 1859 when a farmer in northwestern Pennsylvannia, USA, became the first person to successfully drill for oil. When it is over, it will have lasted less than two centuries.

It is virtually impossible to imagine what the world will be like without oil (see Appendix 2). Without oil, our modern world, with its mass-scale urban existence, will experience recurring dysfunctionality and systems breakdowns.

Within a few years, world demand for oil is going to outstrip supply. Then we will enter a period of continuous hikes and wild fluctuations in the costs of petrol and other sources of energy like gas. We are also likely to see increasing power cuts as industrialised systems begin their long, slow descent into inoperability.

World peak oil is imminent because we have already used half of Earth's total endowment of two trillion barrels of liquid oil. Even an absurdly conservative estimate of when total oil supplies will run out puts oil's Judgment Day, when all supplies will be finished, at the year 2040.[292]

At the current rate of its growth, China alone will consume 100 per cent of currently available world exports in ten years.[293] China is purchasing half a million new cars every year as it charts its course to become a monster-size consumer society and a world superpower. At some point, an unstoppable force – China's growth – will encounter an immovable object: the depletion of oil supplies. The repercussions of that collision will be catastrophic for the world economy and for global peace.

While oil production is heading for permanent decline, humankind's energy needs continue to multiply exponentially. The economic growth rate of China and India together is two or three times higher than that of the United States.[294] One day their consumption of oil will outstrip that of today's superpower. They will more than double their oil consumption within twenty-five years.[295] This is happening at the worst possible time: China's and India's peaks of growth will occur long after oil is in serious decline.

The demand for energy is escalating beyond the world's capacity to meet its requirements. In 1970, the world consumed about 46 million barrels of oil a day (bpd). By 1979, global consumption had grown to over 65 million bpd. Global demand for oil has been increasing at a rate of about 1.5 to 2 million bpd each year: 'The U.S. Department of Energy and the International Energy Agency both project that global oil demand could grow from the current 77 mbd to 120 mbd in 20 years driven by the United States and South and East Asia.'[296]

E Day, when oil reaches Empty, is likely to happen between 2030 and 2050, even with new methods of extraction like fracking: 'The earth's crust contains only so much oil that can be extracted for a reasonable cost, and no amount of money or brains can change that fact. Since there is only a finite number of oil patches in the world, global oil production must eventually decline... Eventually, the costs will exceed the rewards.'[297]

Whether peak oil happens in fifteen or fifty years' time, the fact is that it will happen. And that means three unavoidable consequences will result. First, our vast consumer societies are going to experience profound systemic problems regarding their 'carrying capacity' for sustaining a complex city economy. In other words, as energy sources decrease, power outages increase. Systems of long-range transport and 'just-in-time' delivery of retail goods from all over the world will collapse.

Second, the costs of energy will rise to unheard-of levels. This will generate severe economic effects and social challenges.

And, third, there will be geopolitical struggles, and possible wars, fought over dwindling energy sources. Our civilisation is based on oil and cannot function without it.[298] Without oil, urban and suburban lifestyles will be crippled.

The four revolutions outlined in Table 5 will drive the major changes to be witnessed in this century. Together, they represent a magnitude of fundamental change not yet faced by our young global civilisation. What are we to do? Where are we to turn?

16
Where, then, are we going?

> 'Science, and indeed the whole of civilisation, is a
> series of incremental advances, each building on
> what went before.'
> Stephen Hawking, *On the Shoulders of Giants*
> (2002)

Direction is everything.

The *Titanic* sank because it didn't change direction in time to prevent its fatal collision. Science advances in a common direction, as Hawking suggests, through collective accumulation of knowledge of how the world works. And time itself, physics shows, has a definite direction – it points forwards only. Direction is even more important than destination because most of life is spent evolving, that is, journeying without arrival.

But political governance today is not doing a very good job at finding and maintaining the right direction for society.

In addition, the four fundamental changes of order, or revolutions (see Table 5), by their magnitude alone, are associated with potential for widespread disorder. A global implosion, an epic fall of the globalised world, cannot be ruled out if any of these four revolutions go badly wrong. The risks of destruction will be compounded if feedback loops develop between disorder in the environment, the economy and in social structures.

How can we shift the trajectories of unfolding history away from this worst-case scenario of collapse for the world?

The evolution of society is a deep-rooted process which may be steered. All we need to do to avoid hitting the icebergs ahead is to heed the warnings and then change direction when required. We've seen that the ship of the twenty-first century is heading towards four gigantic icebergs:

- Demographic or biological decline through depopulation and global ageing, with detrimental economic effects.

- Shifts of power and influence in global politics driven by changing demographics.

- Socio-environmental collapses due to exhausted or increasingly inhospitable environments.

- Changes in the industrial energy order with risks of rising costs, economic disruption and conflict.

To respond to four changes of order will demand a new paradigm of human governance. A simple, positive change of direction for global society would be to switch from ideology to science as the guiding ethos for governing modern nation states. Our ship of state is likely to collide with the icebergs if we do not shift direction towards science away from ideology in governance of social, political and economic systems.

Right now, we're in the midst of a planetary emergency. The Doomsday Clock is ticking. Problems like global warming, degradation of land (with its associated loss of fertility for growing crops), and depletion of finite key natural resources like oil, will strain national budgets and resources to the limit. In extreme cases, they will cause drought, famine, starvation, bankruptcy and destruction of whole communities.

Jared Diamond's evocative study *Collapse* shows how past societies which broke down completely, such as the Mayan civilisation in the Americas or the Polynesian culture of Easter Island, did so as a result of environmental catastrophe caused by deforestation, soil erosion, drought, climate change and overexploitation of natural resources, coupled with a blindness on the part of leaders and rulers to read the ominous signs of the times.

On the surface, our global society looks like a rich patchwork quilt of cities and mega-cities stitched together by trade and airline routes, satellite television, cinema and mass media, internet, radio, telecommunications and human migration patterns. The result is the greatest communications and trading network the Earth has ever seen. Hasn't our progress been breathtakingly successful?

Below the surface of our Modern Age, with its great global communications and trading network, the structural foundations are crumbling. This includes the institution of the family (especially marriage and the core role of procreation of the species), social structures, energy supply chains required to power industrial society, and, most damaging of all, the relationship between economies and the planet's underlying ecosystems.

The governance of the world is in tatters, not just because ideology is so deadly in its ineffectiveness and potential for conflict, but due to a failure to address global problems, from climate change to organised crime.[299]

Of the four revolutions discussed in the previous chapter, the one which scares me most as a futurist is the depopulation bomb. It makes my blood run cold to watch fertility and birth rates plummet worldwide to sub-replacement levels. Are we going to stay on the road to extinction by refusing to reproduce ourselves as a species, turning our back on our collective survival in the ultimate act of selfish short-termism?

I fear for nations which are already on course to shrink with every passing year and every new generation. I fear for the global ageing of nations and the human population itself and the havoc depopulation could bring to economies around the world. Once we pass the point of irreversible biological decline of the species, bringing in its wake certain economic decline, there'll be no magic wand to wave to hold back our final demise.

Demographically, it is a near-certainty to me that pro-natal populations, including religious groups and communities, will rise to greater social power in the midst of humanity's general biological decline.

We can still change direction to avoid this slow slide into decay and eventual extinction. There's a system of thought and knowledge, both theoretical and applied, called science, which can outsmart the forces of destruction. As I've argued, the ship of state needs to be guided by science, not ideology.

While progress implies movement towards an ideal, which often gets encapsulated in an ideology embraced by a nation, progression is the continuous movement forward in the right direction. For progress, destination matters most. For progression, direction matters most. Progress can be an ideologically loaded concept. Progression, by contrast, is more neutral in tone. The FutureFinder system, introduced in Chapters 11 to 13, is aimed at pointing individuals, organisations and nations systematically in the right direction to achieve progression, by getting the fundamental factors of the future firmly in place. By being future-facing, we become better aligned with time and the forces of time.

Since time moves exceedingly fast, it will be in short supply as we try to fix the growing disorder accompanying the four revolutions we face in this century. Given this time sensitivity, embracing science as our main framework for governance may not be enough. In addition, it will pay huge dividends to extend science from its current domains in the physical and social sciences into study of the future. This will address the shortcoming that our current knowledge falls incessantly behind the forces of change.

Through futurology we can jump ahead of change, overtake time and stay one step ahead, in control of our destiny. Time is short, time is fast. Soon, only the fast will survive. And the fast are those who see into the future and prepare for it.

The nineteenth century was a century of empires. The twentieth century was the century of ideology. The twenty-first century should be the century of science, including a science of future study.

That means adopting a causal approach to the world – and to the future. Like the rest of reality, the future is caused. The world obeys the laws of nature yesterday, today and tomorrow. We aspire to read the future of the world like a book. But it's written in a code which appears on the surface to be incomprehensible, seemingly shrouded in uncertainty and complexity. Deep below the surface, however, there are systematic processes by which the future is produced. And these are the very same processes which produce everyday reality.

After centuries of sublime efforts and breakthroughs, science has laid bare how life works. It's time to apply laws of nature and methods of scientific study to the future. This will make us powerful, rather than paralysed and powerless, in the face of irresistible change. Bacon foresaw the power that would be unleashed by adopting the scientific method: 'Knowledge and human power are synonymous, since the ignorance of the cause frustrates the effect; for nature is only subdued by submission...'[300]

Kant was adamant that things happen in nature according to law, not chance: 'Hence the proposition, Nothing happens by blind chance (*in mundo non datur casus*), is an *a priori* law of nature.'[301] Necessity in nature is not blind: it's intelligible (*non datur factum*). The intelligible order of nature, laid bare by centuries of scientific investigation, points to a hidden order of the future, too. It is disorder which is the chief source of evil in the world. By contrast, science seeks to impose order on seemingly unintelligible change. For there is order in:

- Space–time
- The solar system
- Nature's systems
- The driving forces of evolution
- The pattern of human nature
- The cycles of history

In addition, the order of the future is part of the order of time, which Hume described as an ordering principle for all existence. We see order in the world. Given time's continuity and sequential order, and its regularity, we need to include the future within the order of reality.

In this book, we've searched for, and found, the future's hidden order by answering these two questions:

- How much of the future is written into nature's rule book?

- How much of the future is written into time's order?

Enlightened by the greatest works of science and philosophy ever written, the hidden order of the future has been unveiled. Given that physics and philosophy have established that the three key properties of time are its direction, its continuity and its sequential nature, it's natural to expect the future to be ultimately knowable.

The future is substantially present all around us in the evolutionary cycles working out their built-in purposes. The past casts a shadow on the present in the form of memories and effects from past events and conditions. Likewise, we can see foreshadows of the future. In the same way that the past creates impressions we call memories, and the present continuously makes sense impressions on us, so too the future creates impressions on the mind called foreshadows. Just as watermarks are subjacent to, or underlying, the main text of graphics on a page, so these mental foreshadows are lighter in form than physical impressions and memories, more like outlines and silhouettes. But these foreshadows are just the beginning of our understanding of the future.

To my mind, the future is just as embedded in the present as the past is.

The fact that life moves forwards fast and changes in one direction only is profoundly favourable for futurists. Here's why. We can observe the flow of time and how things change over time. They change according to the law of causation. Things evolve into their future states from their current state in a structured way following patterns of causation. This enables us to make logical inferences about those future states.

As the great Greek thinker Aristotle believed over twenty-three centuries ago, there's a teleology at work in nature by which living things point towards their end purposes, their goals, fulfilling the functions for which they have been made as they move and change.

Change in our century will be overwhelming due to its phenomenal magnitude. Unless we study the time patterns of everything and plan for their future evolution, unless we follow the trail of causation in every change, we'll fall so far behind change, that we'll be swallowed up by unstoppable forces of disorder and decline.

Continuous progression is our goal. Science is our method. Order is our value. Knowledge-based governance is our model. It's best for civilisation to face in time's direction – forwards.

Confronted by the prospect of eventual biological demise, with a depopulation bomb about to go off in our world, we need to reawaken the desire to survive and to thrive.

Going forward, we can embrace a new cosmic change of consciousness to accompany the current advances in understanding of cosmology, discovering our masterful place in the universe and developing an ambitious plan to colonise outer space. On a small scale, we've started to formulate far-future visions of establishing civilisations on planets beyond the solar system.

Currently, there are no real global plans to preserve life after the sun's death. In the long run, this may have the subconscious effect of undermining the will to survive, something which is already under threat due to worldwide cultural and demographic trends.

So a global priority for future world leaders is to plan the financing of the exploration of space and the search for our extra-terrestrial future, with human settlement on Mars attained before the end of this century as a first stepping stone to a post-solar civilisation.

Without progression, even towards the far future, there'll only be continued decay, adding to the growing problem of biological decline. Pointing in the right direction makes the ship of state confident and strong, even if it'll take millennia to succeed in building settlements on planets outside the solar system. The need to continue the infinite journey to places of human habitation beyond the solar system is a stepping-stone approach to continued existence after the extinction of the sun.

How time becomes the future, and how current states pass into future states through patterns of causation, represents a new frontier of human – and scientific – knowledge. Categorising and accumulating knowledge of the future would empower us to be truly proactive and much more efficient as a species.

The future has a code and it's similar to a computer programme. The code is written in the language of causation. This makes it possible, when employing a systematic causal analysis, to foresee and model the future. In the same way that the discipline of history was created to discover, and learn from, the past, futurology may be grounded as a science which will help us to see the world of tomorrow long before it arrives. I'm sure we're about to become more proactive as a species than we've ever been by an order of magnitude beyond our wildest dreams.

Robert Goddard (1882–1945), the rocket scientist and pioneer of space flight, said: 'It is difficult to say what is impossible, for the dream of yesterday is the hope of today and the reality of tomorrow.'[302]

Destiny is the direction towards order, balance and fulfilment of innate purpose. We become human mainly through our beliefs and our purposes. As we move towards a better, higher state, we find ourselves perpetually energised in the living process of progression.

Notes

Chapter 1

1. Aquinas, *A Summary of Philosophy* (2003) (1265–74) 31.
2. Wolfram, *A New Kind of Science* (2002) 383.
3. Wolfram, *A New Kind of Science* (2002) 1002.
4. Kant, *Critique of Pure Reason* (1998) (1781) 195.
5. Mathematica is described in Wikipedia as a computational software program used in scientific, engineering and mathematical fields and other areas of technical computing – http://en.wikipedia.org/wiki/Mathematica
6. Wolfram, *A New Kind of Science* (2002) 471.
7. Wolfram, *A New Kind of Science* (2002) 720,721.
8. Laplace, *A Philosophical Essay on Probabilities* (1814) 177.
9. Wolfram, *A New Kind of Science* (2002) 5, 715.
10. Wolfram, *A New Kind of Science* (2002) 547.
11. Wolfram, *A New Kind of Science* (2002) 1004.
12. Wolfram, *A New Kind of Science* (2002) 1191–2.
13. Aquinas, *A Summary of Philosophy* (2003) (1265–74) 26.
14. Hume wrote: 'The sciences, which treat of general facts, are politics, natural philosophy, physic, chymistry, etc., where the qualities, causes and effects of a whole species of objects are enquired into.' Hume, *An Enquiry concerning Human Understanding* (2008) (1748) 120.
15. Kant, *Critique of Pure Reason* (1998) (1781) 181.
16. Hawking, *God Created the Integers* (2005) xiii.

Chapter 2

17. See my essay 'The compelling benefits of a scientific approach to South Africa's future' – http://www.futurology.co.za/code/knowing.htm
18. As a general rule of thumb, the short-term future is largely determined by the immediate effects of current reality, including the kinds of

173

technology being used and developed. The medium-term future seems to be determined to a greater extent by the effects of powerful social systems. What produces the far future, though, are universal factors of nature and human nature, including demography and changes to the environment.

19.   Mandela, *Long Walk to Freedom* (1994) 373.

Chapter 3

20.   Hume, *An Enquiry concerning Human Understanding* (2008) (1748) 19.
21.   Kant, *Critique of Human Reason* (1998) (1781) 172.
22.   Hegel, *Encyclopedia of the Philosophical Sciences in Outline and Critical Writings* (1990) 141.
23.   Aquinas, *A Summary of Philosophy* (2003) (1265–74) 4.
24.   Kant, *Critique of Human Reason* (1998) (1781) 380.
25.   Kant, *Critique of Human Reason* (1998) (1781) 386.
26.   Kant, *Critique of Human Reason* (1998) (1781) 381.
27.   Hume, *A Treatise of Human Nature* (1985) (1739–40) 123.
28.   Aquinas, *A Summary of Philosophy* (2003) (1265–74) 25.
29.   Aquinas, *A Summary of Philosophy* (2003) (1265–74) 27, 29.
30.   Aristotle, *Physics* (2008) (350 BC) 50–3.
31.   Aristotle, *Physics* (2008) (350 BC) 54.
32.   Kant, *Critique of Human Reason* (1998) (1781) 129.
33.   Aquinas, *A Summary of Philosophy* (2003) (1265–74) 31.
34.   Aquinas, *A Summary of Philosophy* (2003) (1265–74) 39.
35.   Aristotle understands form as what makes things the kind of thing they are, that is their core characteristics: 'since the end is form, and everything else takes place for the sake of the end, it is this form that is the cause, since it is that for which everything happens'. Aristotle, *Physics* (2008) (350 BC) 52.
36.   Aristotle, *Physics* (2008) (350 BC) 49.
37.   Aristotle, *Physics* (2008) (350 BC) 40.
38.   Aristotle, *Physics* (2008) (350 BC) 56.
39.   Aristotle, *Physics* (2008) (350 BC) 167.
40.   Aristotle, *Physics* (2008) (350 BC) 118.
41.   Aristotle, *Physics* (2008) (350 BC) 119.
42.   Aristotle, *Physics* (2008) (350 BC)196.
43.   Hume, *A Treatise of Human Nature* (1985) (1739–40) 136. He states 'the constant conjunction of objects determines their causation'. Hume, *A Treatise of Human Nature* (1985) (1739–40) 223.
44.   Hume, *A Treatise of Human Nature* (1985) (1739–40) 124. Hume outlined eight rules of causation as follows:
'(1) The cause and effect must be contiguous in space and time. (2) The cause must be prior to the effect. (3) There must be a constant union betwixt the cause and effect. 'Tis chiefly this quality, that constitutes the relation.(4) The same cause always produces the same effect, and the same effect never arises but from the same

cause.... (5) ...where several different objects produce the same effect, it must be by means of some quality, which we discover to be common amongst them.... (6) ... The difference in the effects of two resembling objects must proceed from that particular, in which they differ. For as like causes always produce like effects, when in any instance we find our expectation to be disappointed, we must conclude that this irregularity proceeds from some difference in the causes. (7) When any object increases or diminishes with the increase or diminution of its cause, 'tis to be regarded as a compound effect, derived from the union of the several different effects, which arise from the several different parts of the cause. The absence or presence of one part of the cause is here supposed to be always attended with the absence or presence of a proportional part of the effect. This constant conjunction sufficiently proves, that the one part is the cause of the other .... (8) The eighth and last rule I shall take notice of is, that any object, which exists for any time in its full perfection without any effect, is not the sole cause of that effect, but requires to be assisted by some other principle, which may forward its influence and operation. For as like effects necessarily follow from like causes, and ion a contiguous time and place, their separation for a moment shews, that these causes are not the compleat ones.' Hume, *A Treatise of Human Nature* (1985) (1739–40) 308–9.

45. Descartes, *Meditations and Other Metaphysical Writings* (1998) (1641) 121.

46. Mellor, *The Facts of Causation* (1995) 13.

47. Kant, *Critique of Pure Reason* (1998) (1781) 162.

48. Kant, *Critique of Pure Reason* (1998) (1781) 203.

49. Kant, *Critique of Pure Reason* (1998) (1781) 173.

50. Hume states: 'But when many uniform instances appear, and the same object is always followed by the same event; we then begin to entertain the notion of cause and connexion.' Hume, *An Enquiry concerning Human Understanding* (2008) (1748), 56–7. He also explains causation in these words: 'our idea, therefore, of necessity and causation arises entirely from the uniformity, observable in the operations of nature; where similar objects are constantly conjoined together, and the mind is determined by custom to infer the one from the appearance of the other ... beyond the constant conjunction of similar objects, and the consequent inference from one to the other, we have no notion of any necessity, or connexion.' Hume, *An Enquiry concerning Human Understanding* (2008) (1748) 59–60.

51. Kant, *Critique of Pure Reason* (1998) (1781) 129.

52. Kant, *Critique of Pure Reason* (1998) (1781) 385.

53. Kant, *Critique of Pure Reason* (1998) (1781) 184.

54. Kant, *Critique of Pure Reason* (1998) (1781) 59.

55. Hume, *A Treatise of Human Nature* (1985) (1739–40) 139.

56. Hume, *An Enquiry concerning Human Understanding* (2008) (1748) 59.

57. Kant, *Critique of Pure Reason* (1998) (1781) 44.

58. Paul & Hall, *Causation: A User's Guide* (2013), 4.

59. Paul & Hall, *Causation: A User's Guide* (2013) 1.

60. Paul & Hall, *Causation: A User's Guide* (2013) 4.

61. Kant, *Critique of Pure Reason* (1998) (1781) 386.

62. Kant, *Critique of Pure Reason* (1998) (1781) 385.

63. Albert Einstein, Foreword to *Dialogue Concerning the two Chief World Systems* by Galileo Gallilei. Galileo (2012) (1632) xxiii.

64. Kant, *Critique of Pure Reason* (1998) (1781) 386.

65. Kant, *Critique of Pure Reason* (1998) (1781) 387.

66. Kant discusses the case of someone telling a lie. Although the action of lying may have been determined by a range of background circumstances such as bad company the person may have been keeping or the personal problems he may have been having, he's still culpable for the action, because he's a free agent who chose to lie, and it was *reason* which was the cause of the action. Kant, *Critique of Pure Reason* (1998) (1781) 387–8.

67. Aristotle, *Physics* (2008) (350 BC) 49.

68. Aristotle, *Physics* (2008) (350 BC) 120.

69. Hegel saw causes producing effects which themselves activate another causal impact: 'The cause, which has an effect, is itself an effect, but not of a cause that lies behind and beyond its own effect, rather of a cause that arises in the first place within its own effect.' Hegel, *Encyclopedia of the Philosophical Sciences in Outline and Critical Writings* (1990) 98. It seems that the cause changes the dependent entity through its effects and activates causal influences to produce yet another effect in the endless chain of cause and effect.

70. Hume stated: 'The necessary connexion betwixt causes and effects is the foundation of our inference from one to the other. The foundation of our inference is the transition arising from the accustom'd union.' Hume, *A Treatise of Human Nature* (1985) (1739–40) 216.

71. Pearsall, ed., *New Oxford Dictionary of English* (1998) 936.

72. Pearsall, ed., *New Oxford Dictionary of English* (1998) 1454.

73. Hume, *A Treatise of Human Nature* (1985) (1739–40) 138.

74. Hume, *A Treatise of Human Nature* (1985) (1739–40) 330. Hume sees all these terms as almost synonymous: efficacy, agency, power, force, energy, necessity, connection and productive quality and they are all terms essential to the definition of causation (Hume, *A Treatise of Human Nature* (1985) (1739–40) 206).

75. Hume, *A Treatise of Human Nature* (1985) (1739–40) 225.

76. Hume, *A Treatise of Human Nature* (1985) (1739–40) 475.

77. Hume stated: 'When we infer any particular cause from an effect, we must proportion the one to the other, and can never be allowed to ascribe to the cause any qualities, but what are exactly sufficient to produce the effect… But if we ascribe to it farther qualities, or affirm it capable of producing other effects, we can only indulge the licence of conjecture, and arbitrarily suppose the existence of qualities and energies, without reason or authority.' Hume, *An Enquiry concerning Human Understanding* (2008) (1748) 99. He provides the following caveat; 'If the cause be known only by the effect, we never ought to ascribe to it any qualities, beyond what are precisely requisite to produce the effect.' Hume, *An Enquiry concerning Human*

Understanding (2008) (1748) 99. In short, he argues: 'The cause must be proportioned to the effect...' Hume, *An Enquiry concerning Human Understanding* (2008) (1748) 99.

78. Newton, *The Principia* (1995) (1687), 320.
79. Aristotle, *Physics* (2008) (350 BC) 170.
80. Aquinas, *A Summary of Philosophy* (2003) (1265–74) 93–4.
81. Kant, *Critique of Pure Reason* (1998) (1781) 386.
82. Hume, *An Enquiry concerning Human Understanding* (2008) (1748) 66.
83. Kant, *Critique of Pure Reason* (1998) (1781) 382.
84. Kant, *Critique of Pure Reason* (1998) (1781) 184.
85. Kant, *Critique of Pure Reason* (1998) (1781) 185.
86. Paul & Hall, *Causation: A User's Guide* (2013) 18.

Chapter 4

87. Aristotle, *Physics* (2008) (350 BC) 111.
88. Aristotle stated: '...how could there be such a thing as time if there is no such thing as change?' Aristotle, *Physics* (2008) (350 BC) 187.
89. Aristotle, *Physics* (2008) (350 BC) 39.
90. Aristotle, *Physics* (2008) (350 BC) 116.
91. Aristotle, *Physics* (2008) (350 BC) 56.
92. Aristotle stated: '...time is a measure of change ... what it is for it [any entity] to be in time is for its existence to be measured by time'. Aristotle, *Physics* (2008) (350 BC) 109–10.
93. Aristotle, *Physics* (2008) (350 BC) 62.
94. Aristotle, *Physics* (2008) (350 BC) 104. The great philosopher also stated: 'time seems to be everywhere...' Aristotle, *Physics* (2008) (350 BC) 115.
95. Kant, *Critique of Pure Reason* (1998) (1781) 56–7.
96. Aristotle, *Physics* (2008) (350 BC) 111.
97. Aristotle, *Physics* (2008) (350 BC) 105.
98. Aristotle, *Physics* (2008) (350 BC) 142.
99. Aristotle, *Physics* (2008) (350 BC) 112–13.
100. Aristotle, *Physics* (2008) (350 BC) 113.

Chapter 5

101. Hegel, *Phenomenology of Spirit* (1977) (1807) 3–4.
102. Kant, *Critique of Pure Reason* (1998) (1781) 6.
103. Kant, *Critique of Pure Reason* (1998) (1781) 42.
104. In Hawking, *God Created the Integers* (2005) 704.
105. Kant, *Critique of Pure Reason* (1998) (1781) 198.
106. 'All bodies whatsoever are endowed with a principle of mutual gravitation.' Newton, *The Principia* (1995) (1687) 321.
107. Hawking, *The Grand Design* (2010) 27.

108. Jackson, *The Elements: An Illustrated History of the Periodic Table* (2012) 73.
109. Hume, *An Enquiry concerning Human Understanding* (2008) (1748) 66.
110. Hume, *An Enquiry concerning Human Understanding* (2008) (1748) 64.
111. Hume, *A Treatise of Human Nature* (1985) (1739–40) 310.
112. Hume, *A Treatise of Human Nature* (1985) (1739–40) 309.
113. Hume, *An Enquiry concerning Human Understanding* (2008) (1748) 60.
114. Hume, *A Treatise of Human Nature* (1985) (1739–40) 347–8.
115. Hume, *An Enquiry concerning Human Understanding* (2008) (1748) 65.
116. Hume described the human body as 'a mighty complicated machine'. Hume, *An Enquiry concerning Human Understanding* (2008) (1748) 63.

Chapter 6

117. Hacking, *An Introduction to Probability and Inductive Logic* (2001) in Chapter 4 'Elementary Probability Ideas'.
118. Keynes, *A Treatise on Probability* (1920), Chapter 1 'The Meaning of Probability'.
119. Laplace, *A Philosophical Essay on Probabilities* (1814) 7–8.
120. Hawking, *God Created the Integers* (2005) 394.
121. Laplace, *A Philosophical Essay on Probabilities* (1814) 11.
122. Laplace, *A Philosophical Essay on Probabilities* (1814) 17.
123. Laplace, *A Philosophical Essay on Probabilities* (1814) 3.
124. Hume, *An Enquiry concerning Human Understanding* (2008) (1748) 69.
125. Pearsall, ed., *The New Oxford Dictionary of English* (1998) 1563.
126. Laplace, *A Philosophical Essay on Probabilities* (1814) 4. He believed in a proven cosmic order, based on the law of universal gravity and other laws of nature.
127. Hawking, *God Created the Integers* (2005) 399. 'In a series of probable events of which the ones produce a benefit and the others a loss, we shall have the advantage which results from it by making a sum of the products of the probability of each favourable event by the benefit which it procures, and subtracting from this sum that of the products of the probability of each unfavourable event by the loss attached to it. If the second sum is greater than the first, the benefit becomes a loss and hope is changed to fear.' Hawking, *God Created the Integers* (2005) 400.
128. Laplace, *A Philosophical Essay on Probabilities* (1814) 22.
129. Hawking, *God Created the Integers* (2005) 470–1. 'It is principally at games of chance that a multitude of illusions support hope and sustain it against unfavourable chances. The majority of those who play at lotteries do not know how many chances are to their advantage, how many are contrary to them. They see only the possibility by a small stake of gaining a considerable sum and the projects which their imagination brings forth, exaggerate to their eyes the probability of obtaining it.' Hawking, *God Created the Integers* (2005) 471.
130. Galileo, *Selected Writings* (2012) 78.

131. Hawking, *God Created the Integers* (2005) 482.
132. 'The celestial phenomena, compared with the laws of motion, conduct us, therefore, to this great principle of nature, namely, that all the molecules of matter mutually attract each other in the proportion of their masses, divided by the square of their distances.' Laplace, *A Treatise of Celestial Mechanics* (1822) Part 1, Book 11, 24–5.
133. Reichenbach, *The Rise of Scientific Philosophy* (1951) 252.
134. Reichenbach, *The Rise of Scientific Philosophy* (1951) 249.
135. Reichenbach, *The Rise of Scientific Philosophy* (1951) 246: 'To control the future – to shape future happenings according to a plan – presupposes predictive knowledge of what will happen if certain conditions are realized … the justification of induction is that it is the best instrument of action known to us.'
136. Reichenbach, *The Rise of Scientific Philosophy* (1951) 233.
137. Reichenbach, *The Rise of Scientific Philosophy* (1951) 236, 246.
138. Laplace stated: 'If we should try all the hypotheses which can be formed in regard to the cause of phenomena we should arrive, by a process of exclusion, at the true one.' Laplace, *A Philosophical Essay on Probabilities* (1814) 183.

Chapter 7

139. Wolfram, *A New Kind of Science* (2002) 1187.
140. Wolfram, *A New Kind of Science* (2002) 973.
141. Strogatz, *Sync: the emerging science of spontaneous order* (2003) 184.
142. Richeson, *Euler's Gem – the polyhedron formula and the birth of topology* (2008) 2.
143. 'Dung beetles navigate by the stars', 25 January 2013, *Guardian*. http://www.guardian.co.uk/science/2013/jan/25/dung-beetles-navigate-stars The researchers say their findings represent the first proven use of the Milky Way for orientation in the animal kingdom: 'African ball-rolling dung beetles exploit the sun, the moon, and the celestial polarization pattern to move along straight paths, away from the intense competition at the dung pile. Even on clear moonless nights, many beetles still manage to orientate along straight paths. This led us to hypothesize that dung beetles exploit the starry sky for orientation, a feat that has, to our knowledge, never been demonstrated in an insect. Here, we show that dung beetles transport their dung balls along straight paths under a starlit sky but lose this ability under overcast conditions. In a planetarium, the beetles orientate equally well when rolling under a full starlit sky as when only the Milky Way is present.' *Current Biology*. Volume 23, Issue 4, 18 February 2013, Pages 298–300. 'Dung Beetles Use the Milky Way for Orientation', by Marie Dacke, Emily Baird, Marcus Byrne, Clarke H. Scholtz, Eric J. Warrant.
144. Strogatz, *Sync: the emerging science of spontaneous order* (2003) 14.
145. Strogatz, *Sync: the emerging science of spontaneous order* (2003) 15.
146. Strogatz, *Sync: the emerging science of spontaneous order* (2003) 69. The synchrony behind the circadian rhythm occurs on three levels,

according to Strogatz, (i) cells within an organ are synchronized; (ii) organs are synchronised within the body, and (iii) the body itself synchronises to the world and its 24-hour cycle (Strogatz: 72). There is, it seems, a circadian code and a circadian clock.

147. Wolfram, *A New Kind of Science* (2002)1098.
148. Strogatz, *Sync: the emerging science of spontaneous order* (2003) 14.
149. Hume, *A Treatise of Human Nature* (1985) (1739–40) 181.
150. Laplace, *A Philosophical Essay on Probabilities* (1814) 60.
151. Laplace, *A Philosophical Essay on Probabilities* (1814) 62.
152. Aristotle, *Physics*, (2008) (350 BC) 56.
153. Pearsall, ed., *The New Oxford Dictionary of English* (1998) 456.
154. Crystal, *The Cambridge Encyclopedia* (2000) 649.
155. Winter is unlikely to ever come after spring. Seasons are not going to get significantly longer in duration. We're not going to age in reverse. The sun will never orbit the Earth and the moon won't exert a greater gravitational force than our home planet. The Gulf Stream, which brings temperate weather to Europe, isn't going to switch off overnight. Henry Ford's Model T isn't ever going to be a bestselling motor vehicle again (although other models will follow a similar path of exponential growth to a peak of production, followed by relatively sharp decline). Oil is never going to get progressively cheaper. Japan's population is not suddenly going to start getting younger. October isn't going to regularly attract higher retail sales than traditional December spending sprees. Stocks aren't suddenly going to flatten out into linear progressions.
156. Aristotle, *Physics* (2008) (350 BC) 117.
157. Winfree, *The Timing of Biological Clocks* (1987) 12, 42, 145.
158. Winfree, *The Timing of Biological Clocks* (1987) 160.
159. Toynbee, *A Study of History* Volumes 1–V1 (1946) 45.
160. Toynbee, *A Study of History* Volumes 1–V1 (1946) 51.
161. Toynbee, *A Study of History* Volumes 1–V1 (1946) 49.
162. Toynbee, *A Study of History* Volumes 1–V1 (1946) 75.
163. Toynbee believed that 'ease is inimical to civilisation' (Toynbee, *A Study of History* Volumes 1–V1 (1946) 88); only in challenging conditions could a civilisation thrive.
164. Toynbee, *A Study of History* Volumes 1–V1 (1946) 187.
165. Toynbee, *A Study of History* Volumes 1–V1 (1946) 189.
166. Toynbee, *A Study of History* Volumes 1–V1 (1946) 548.
167. Toynbee, *A Study of History* Volumes 1–V1 (1946) 198.
168. Toynbee stated: 'If, as we have been led to think, self-determination is the criterion of growth, and if self-determination means self-articulation, we shall be analysing the process by which civilizations actually grow if we investigate the way in which they progressively articulate themselves.' Toynbee, *A Study of History* Volumes 1–V1 (1946) 206, 208.
169. Toynbee, *A Study of History* Volumes 1–V1 (1946) 214–15.
170. Toynbee, *A Study of History* Volumes 1–V1 (1946) 215. He states: 'human nature never changes'.

171. Toynbee, *A Study of History* Volumes 1–V1 (1946) 253.

172. Toynbee, *A Study of History* Volumes 1–V1 (1946) 254.

173. Toynbee, *A Study of History* Volumes 1–V1 (1946) 589.

174. Toynbee, *A Study of History* Volumes V11–X (1957) 276.

175. Toynbee, *A Study of History* Volumes 1–V1 (1946) 556.

176. Toynbee defines growth and disintegration as applied to civilisation in these words: 'A growing civilization can be defined as one in which the components of its culture – the economic, political and the "cultural" in the stricter sense – are in harmony with one another; and, on the same principle, a disintegrating civilization can be defined as one in which these three elements have fallen into discord.' Toynbee, *A Study of History* Volumes V11–X (1957) 122–3.

177. Toynbee, *A Study of History* Volumes 1–V1 (1946) 246.

178. Toynbee, *A Study of History* Volumes 1–V1 (1946) 276. 'Of the twenty-one civilizations that have been born alive and have proceeded to grow, thirteen are dead and buried; that seven of the remaining eight are apparently in decline; and that the eighth, which is our own, may also have passed its zenith … the career of a growing civilization would appear to be fraught with danger.'

179. Toynbee describes this breakdown in these words: 'This secession of the led from the leaders may be regarded as a loss of harmony between the parts which make up the whole ensemble of the society. In any whole consisting of parts a loss of harmony between the parts is paid for by the whole in a corresponding loss of self-determination. This loss of self-determination is the ultimate criterion of breakdown; and it is a conclusion which should not surprise us, seeing that it is the inverse of the conclusion … that progress towards self-determination is the criterion of growth.' Toynbee, *A Study of History* Volumes 1–V1 (1946) 279. These breakdowns can, of course, become violent: 'Revolutions are violent because they are the belated triumphs of powerful new social forces over tenacious old institutions which have been temporarily thwarting and cramping these new expressions of life. The longer the obstruction holds out the greater becomes the pressure of the force whose outlet is being obstructed; and the greater the pressure, the more violent the explosion in which the imprisoned force ultimately breaks through.' Toynbee, *A Study of History* Volumes 1–V1 (1946) 281. Militarism of a society is a common feature of this deep disjunction between leaders and their populations.

180. Toynbee, *A Study of History* Volumes 1–V1 (1946) 365.

181. Toynbee, *A Study of History* Volumes V11–X (1957) 284.

182. Toynbee, *A Study of History* Volumes V11–X (1957) 277–9. This respected theoretical historian, however, was not sure of the origin of these laws, saying, 'The laws governing them may be either laws current in man's non-human environment imposing themselves on the course of history from the outside, or they may be laws inherent in the psychic structure and working of human nature itself.' Toynbee, *A Study of History* Volumes V11–X (1957) 279.

183. Toynbee, *A Study of History* Volumes V11–X (1957) 287.

184. Galbraith, *The Great Crash 1929* (1954) 51.

185. Galbraith, *The Great Crash 1929* (1954) 32–3.
186. Galbraith, *The Great Crash 1929* (1954) 96–7.
187. Galbraith, *The Great Crash 1929* (1954) 111.
188. Galbraith, *The Great Crash 1929* (1954) 192.
189. Galbraith, *The Great Crash 1929* (1954) 121.
190. Galbraith, *The Great Crash 1929* (1954) 125.
191. Galbraith, *The Great Crash 1929* (1954) 163.
192. Galbraith, *The Great Crash 1929* (1954) 186.
193. Galbraith, *The Great Crash 1929* (1954) 188.
194. Galbraith, *The Great Crash 1929* (1954) 188–9.
195. Galbraith, *The Great Crash 1929* (1954) 190.
196. Galbraith, *A History of Economics – The Past as the Present* (1987) 263.
197. Galbraith, *A History of Economics – The Past as the Present* (1987) 264.
198. Galbraith, *A History of Economics – The Past as the Present* (1987) 282.
199. Galbraith, *A History of Economics – The Past as the Present* (1987) 292.
200. Galbraith, *A History of Economics – The Past as the Present* (1987) 299.

Chapter 8

201. Longman, *The Empty Cradle* (2004) xiii.
202. Magnus, *The Age of Ageing* (2009) 114.
203. Longman, *The Empty Cradle* (2004) 7.
204. Longman, *The Empty Cradle* (2004) 178
205. It has been argued that the phrase 'Demography is destiny' first appeared in Ben Wattenberg and Richard M. Scammon's 1970 book *The Real Majority: An Extraordinary Examination of the American Electorate* in which the authors paraphrased the saying of Heraclitus (535 BC–475 BC) that 'character is destiny'. They meant that the demographics of a population indicate which political party will prevail in that area.
206. Longman, *The Empty Cradle* (2004) 16.
207. Longman explains: 'But as the cost of pensions and health care consume more and more of the nation's wealth, and as growth of the labor force vanishes, it will become more and more difficult for the United States to sustain its current levels of military spending, let alone maintain today's force levels... Already countries such as Argentina, Brazil, and the former Soviet Union have been deeply destabilised by financial crises largely induced by the unaffordable cost of their pension schemes... China's political and economic system will also be under deep strain due to population ageing, as will that of Japan and Korea, while Europe's social cohesion could also be undone by changing demography.' Longman, *The Empty Cradle* (2004) 20. 'By 2030, according to the Congressional Budget Office, the three big senior benefit programs (Social Security, Medicare and Medicaid) plus interest on the national debt may well consume as much as 24 percent of Gross Domestic Product. By 2050, their cost could well rise to 47 percent of GDP... Without dramatic cuts in benefits or increases in taxes, all federal spending will eventually go to seniors...

The Pentagon today spends 84 cents on pensions for every dollar it spends on basic pay.' Longman, *The Empty Cradle* (2004) 21. So looking into the future of the US for the rest of the century, it looks like demography will stifle its destiny, with declines in demographic and economic health leading to a loss of military power and world influence.

208. Longman, *The Empty Cradle* (2004) 4.
209. Longman, *The Empty Cradle* (2004) 4.
210. Longman, *The Empty Cradle* (2004) 19.
211. Longman, *The Empty Cradle* (2004) 22.
212. Longman, *The Empty Cradle* (2004) 5. Longman states: 'A nation's gross domestic product is literally the sum of its labour force times the average output per worker. Thus, a decline in the number of workers implies a decline in an economy's growth potential... The European Commission ... projects that Europe's potential growth rate over the next fifty years will fall by 40 percent due to the shrinking size of the European work force.' Longman, *The Empty Cradle* (2004). 41. He further elaborates as follows: 'Exploding health and pension costs, along with a shrinking tax base, diminish resources available to households, government, and the private sector for investing in the next generation, even as the need for human capital formation increases. Another reason is rooted in the realities of the life cycle. It's not just that most technological breakthroughs and entrepreneurial activity tend to come from people in their 20s and 30s ... an ageing population will likely become increasingly risk averse...' Longman, *The Empty Cradle* (2004) 43.
213. http://www.investopedia.com/terms/h/humancapital.asp
214. Longman, *The Empty Cradle* (2004) 134–5.
215. Longman, *The Empty Cradle* (2004)190.
216. 'Yet the adults who sacrifice the most to create and mould this precious human capital, whether they be dutiful parents, day care workers, school teachers, camp counsellors, or even college professors, retain only a small share of the value they create. Indeed, as a rule, the more involved one becomes in the nurturing of the next generation, the less compensation one is likely to receive.' Longman, *The Empty Cradle* (2004) 136.
217. Longman states: 'population ageing will cause many pension systems to fold or collapse'. Longman, *The Empty Cradle* (2004) 192.
218. Longman, *The Empty Cradle* (2004) 191.
219. Longman, *The Empty Cradle* (2004) 145.
220. Magnus, *The Age of Ageing* (2009) 33.
221. Magnus, *The Age of Ageing* (2009) 40.
222. Longman, *The Empty Cradle* (2004) 61.
223. Longman, *The Empty Cradle* (2004) 177.
224. Longman, *The Empty Cradle* (2004) 67.
225. Magnus, *The Age of Ageing* (2009) 158.
226. Longman, *The Empty Cradle* (2004) 32.
227. Longman, *The Empty Cradle* (2004) 11.

228. Magnus, *The Age of Ageing* (2009) xxi–xxii.
229. Longman, *The Empty Cradle* (2004) 26.
230. Longman, *The Empty Cradle* (2004) 27.
231. 'When the economic and social incentives to procreate and raise families are weak or negative, as they increasingly are in most nations, and when people know how to achieve sexual gratification without producing children, we have no reason to assume that birth-rates won't continue to fall below replacement level.' Longman, *The Empty Cradle* (2004) 87. 'The economic burden to parents of raising a typical middle class child in the United States through age 18 now exceeds one million dollars in direct costs and foregone wages.'
232. Magnus, *The Age of Ageing* (2009) 42.
233. Longman found that fertility rates in Brazil declined when TV was introduced. 'Today, the number of hours a Brazilian woman spends watching ... domestically produced soap operas, strongly predicts how many children she will have.' Longman, *The Empty Cradle* (2004) 32.
234. 'The key features of today's low or falling fertility rates are: (a) that it is pretty much universal and (b) that, for the first time, it's mostly voluntary. The global nature of low fertility speaks to the combination of several common factors such as faster economic growth, improvements in female literacy and job opportunities and the greater availability of safe, cheap, and legal methods of birth control.' Magnus, *The Age of Ageing* (2009) 41.
235. Magnus, *The Age of Ageing* (2009) 2.
236. Magnus, *The Age of Ageing* (2009) 169.
237. Magnus, *The Age of Ageing* (2009) 18.
238. Longman, *The Empty Cradle* (2004) 35.

Chapter 9

239. 'a particular form of procedure for accomplishing or approaching something, especially a systematic or established one'. Pearsall, ed., *The New Oxford Dictionary of English* (1998) 1164.
240. Climate cycles of hotter and colder periods, cycles of day and night, the seasons themselves, economic cycles, including boom and bust bubbles, production cycles, even cycles of life and death.
241. Ayres explained the driving force behind economic growth in these words: 'the radical improvement in energy conversion possibilities, as represented by the introduction of steam piston engines, steam turbines, gasoline and diesel engines, gas turbines, and electric power, have had ... far-reaching impacts on economic growth ... [leading] to sharp decreases in the cost of primary products (such as iron and steel, aluminum, and plastics) and in "useful work" ... declining costs result in declining prices, increased demand, and increasing scale of production ... which push costs down further. This cyclic scheme [is] ... the primary "engine" of economic growth'. Eds Simpson, Toman & Ayres, *Scarcity and Growth Revisited* (2005) 145. What drives this virtuous circle, then, in this view is that prices of goods

reflect their costs and these prices determine consumption levels. Consumption levels, in turn, drive economies of scale in production. Furthermore, energy efficiency in the production process will impact on these underlying costs. Ayres defines efficiency as the 'ratio of "useful" outputs to inputs', or the ratio of actual work done to the maximum theoretical possible work output, while power is defined as 'work per unit time'. Technical progress itself he equates with increasing efficiency of converting raw resources like coal and oil into useful work. He asserts that energy-to-work conversion efficiency is fundamental to production and accounts for the main contribution of technological progress to economic growth.

242. Moore, *Economic Cycles: their Law and Cause* (1914) 38.
243. Moore, *Economic Cycles: their Law and Cause* (1914) 42.
244. Moore, *Economic Cycles: their Law and Cause* (1914) 30, 40.
245. Descartes wrote: 'I decided that I would observe stubbornly an order in seeking knowledge of things so that, always beginning from the most simple and easy things, I would never proceed to others until it seemed that I could hope for nothing more from them.' Descartes, *Discourse on Method and Related Writings* (1998) (1637) 130.
246. Descartes, *Discourse on Method and Related Writings* (1998) (1637) 131.
247. Descartes, *Discourse on Method and Related Writings* (1998) (1637) 135.
248. Descartes, *Discourse on Method and Related Writings* (1998) (1637) 117–18.
249. Descartes, *Discourse on Method and Related Writings* (1998) (1637) 44.
250. Reichenbach, *The Rise of Scientific Philosophy* (1951) 5.
251. Descartes, *Discourse on Method and Related Writings* (1998) (1637) 59.
252. Descartes, *Discourse on Method and Related Writings* (1998) (1637) 16.

Chapter 10

253. Hume, *A Treatise of Human Nature* (1985) (1739–40) 88.
254. Hume, *A Treatise of Human Nature* (1985) (1739–40) 80.
255. Hume, *A Treatise of Human Nature* (1985) (1739–40) 476–7.
256. Bacon, *The Physical and Metaphysical Works: Including the Advancement of Learning and Novum Organum* (1620) 440.
257. Kant, *Critique of Pure Reason* (1998) (1781) 544.
258. Pearsall, ed., *The New Oxford Dictionary of English* (1998) 932.

Chapter 12

259. Pearsall, ed., *The New Oxford Dictionary of English* (1998) 1307.
260. http://en.wikipedia.org/wiki/Systems_science. Systems sciences are scientific disciplines partly based on systems thinking such as chaos theory, complex systems, control theory, cybernetics, sociotechnical systems theory, systems biology, systems ecology, systems psychology and the already mentioned systems dynamics, systems engineering and systems theory.

261. Wikipedia has an excellent definition of a system: 'A system is composed of interrelated parts or components (structures) that cooperate in processes (behavior). Natural systems include biological entities, ocean currents, the climate, the solar system and ecosystems. Designed systems include airplanes, software systems, technologies and machines of all kinds, government agencies and business systems.' http://en.wikipedia.org/wiki/Systems_thinking

262. See the Benefit Corporation concept explained on the Benefit Corporation Standards Institute website at http://www.bcorpinstitute.org/

Chapter 13

263. 'The Future We Want' – http://www.un.org/en/sustainablefuture/

Chapter 14

264. Bacon, *The Physical and Metaphysical Works Including the Advancement of Learning and Novum Organum* (1620) 434.

265. Laplace, *A Philosophical Essay on Probabilities* (1814) 164.

266. Hume, *A Treatise of Human Nature* (1985) (1739–40) 478–9.

Chapter 15

267. http://www.bpas.org. Bpas, established in 1968, uses business science language to describe its destruction of unborn babies – it is providing an affordable service, it is Britain's largest abortion provider, it provides 'high-quality' abortion care, the demand for home abortions is rising, it has a 'strategy' for enabling twenty-first-century women to maintain control of their lives, motherhood is merely an 'option' and women are free to decide on their own 'priorities', abortion is a 'solution' for unwanted pregnancies. The mother's 'right' to terminate life inside her womb has become a consumer choice. This organisation audaciously calls itself a 'national charity'.

268. 'DIY Abortion Culture', 29 May 2006, Sky News.com – http://www.sky.com/skynews/article/0,,30000-1223068,00.html

269. Buchanan, *The Death of the West* (2002) 13.

270. Buchanan, *The Death of the West* (2002) 22–3.

271. Prestowitz, *Three Billion New Capitalists – the great shift of wealth and power to the East* (2005) 247.

272. Figures supplied by www.DivorceMagazine.com

273. 'Divorce rate highest since 1996', BBC News – UK Edition, 31 August 2005 – http://news.bbc.co.uk/1/hi/uk/4200410.stm

274. For example, in the USA in 1995, the percentage of women whose parents were divorced who themselves went on to get divorced within ten years of marriage was 43 per cent, compared to 29 per cent for women whose parents had stayed together. In 1996, children

of divorce were 50 per cent more likely than their counterparts from intact families to divorce.

275. Married couples have much lower suicide rates than single individuals. 'Special Facts About Suicide' – Suicide Reference Library http://www.suicidereferencelibrary.com

276. By contrast, successful marriages can allow for an unspectacular, but steady, accumulation of assets and wealth, which can then be passed on to the next generation.

277. 'Civitas was launched early in 2000 as an independent registered charity. It is politically non-partisan and ... accepts no government funding. The underlying purpose of Civitas is to deepen public understanding of the legal, institutional and moral framework that makes a free and democratic society possible.' (http://www.civitas.org. uk)

278. Once again, we see how rapidly value paradigm shifts can occur in modern mass societies. They happen at the same speed at which fashions come and go, and travel along the self-same mass distribution channels.

279. In 1970, there were 523,000 unmarried couples living together in the USA. That figure had risen to over 5.5 million cohabiting couples by 2002. This constitutes a 1,000 per cent increase within the span of one generation. Even taking into account population growth between 1970–2002, this increase is colossal, showing a sea-change of attitudes of couples to marriage. In addition, the 2000 US census shows that single Americans who alive alone now make up 26 per cent of all households, more than a quarter of all homes.

280. Cohabitations on average last less than two years before breaking up or converting to marriage and less than 4 per cent of them last for ten years or more.

281. 'Domestic abusers face crackdown', BBC News.com, 3 December 2003 – http://news.bbc.co.uk/1/hi/uk_politics/3254466.stm

282. 'What is domestic violence?' Refuge – http://www.refuge.org.uk/aboutdomesticviolence.html

283. The charity Refuge uses the following definition of domestic violence: 'Domestic violence is the abuse of one partner within an intimate or family relationship. It is the repeated, random and habitual use of intimidation to control a partner. The abuse can be physical, emotional, psychological, financial or sexual. If you are forced to alter your behaviour because you are frightened of your partner's reaction, you are being abused.' 'What is domestic violence?' Refuge – http://www.refuge.org.uk/aboutdomesticviolence.html

284. 'Until Death Do Us Part' *Time Europe Magazine* Special Report, 4 August, 2003 http://www.time.com/time/europe/html/030811/violence/story_4.html

285. 'Domestic Violence Facts', The National Coalition Against Domestic Violence, www.ncadv.org

286. A symbolic Doomsday Clock was first established in 1947 by the *Bulletin of the Atomic Scientists*, founded by former Manhattan Project physicists. BAS has campaigned for nuclear disarmament since 1947.

Its purpose was to reflect the imminence of nuclear annihilation. The Chicago office of BAS keeps a representation of the timepiece. It was first positioned at seven minutes to the hour; since then, it has been changed eighteen times to signify threats to global security. It advanced to two minutes before midnight – its closest proximity to doom – in 1953 after the United States and the Soviet Union detonated hydrogen bombs. 'Climate resets "Doomsday Clock"', by Molly Bentley, 17 January 2007, BBC News.com http://news.bbc.co.uk/1/hi/sci/tech/6270871.stm

287. The scale of natural disasters is now truly vast. 'For 1987–1998, the average number of hydro-meteorological disasters reported was 195; for the years 2000–2006, this number increased by 187% to an average of 365.' (Annual Disaster Statistical Review: Numbers and Trends 2006, p. 21.) And between 2000–06, geological disasters increased by 136 per cent from 1987–98. In 2005, the Paris-based International Council for Science, one of the world's oldest NGOs, stated that the frequency of recorded natural disasters has been rising rapidly. Without any doubt, this century will witness mammoth droughts, floods, tsunamis and windstorms. The Centre for Research on the Epidemiology of Disasters (CRED) reports that between 1974 and 2003, there were 6,367 natural disasters which affected a staggering 5.1 billion people, a number equivalent to over 80 per cent of the human race. These disasters killed more than 2 million people and left 182 million homeless. All the wrong kind of weather records are being broken continuously as we read in the weekly news – worst droughts ever, worst winter storm for 50 years, worst floods ever, worst hurricane season, worst earthquake in decades, etc. In 2002 alone a drought affected 300 million in India, while in China, 100 million were victims of a windstorm, 60 million suffered from a severe drought and a further 60 million were flood victims. Natural disasters cost an average of US$67 billion annually.

288. 'Annual Disaster Statistical Review: Numbers and Trends, 2006' by The Centre for Research on the Epidemiology of Disasters (CRD), Brussels, May 2007, p.13.

289. UN Radio – http://www.un.org/radio/story.asp?NewsID=3462

290. Even the supply of water, the basis of all life, is endangered in some countries. Many of the world's biggest rivers, for example, are under stress from pollution, lower rainfall and overexploitation for irrigation, such as the Ganges, Indus, Nile, Yangtze and Danube. Professor Jeffrey Sachs, director of the UN's Millennium Project, warns that the Ganges has stopped flowing and that radical plans are needed to avert a worldwide shortage of water. The world's longest and most mythic river, the Nile, has served as a source of drinking water for thousands of years but, according to the WWF, it will face scarcity by 2025. The World Business Council on Sustainable Development commissioned a 2006 study on the future availability of water, which was three years in the making. They found that conflict over scarce water is likely to become more common in the world. The International Water Management Institute, the world's leading body on fresh water management, states that global water use has increased six times in the past hundred years and will double again by 2050. Water is needed for domestic, agricultural, industry and energy production use.

Shortages can be economically crippling. If river systems collapse, millions lose their livelihood and food security is threatened. Food production is under threat from both scarcer water supplies and deteriorating fertility of agricultural ground. The International Water Management Institute say demand for food is expected to increase by 50 per cent over the next twenty years due to population increases and improved standards of living in China and India. But will there be enough water to grow the crops that meet this demand for food? If not, there will be increased starvation on a potentially mass scale.

291. 'Climate change fight can't wait', BBC.News.com, 31 October 2006 – http://news.bbc.co.uk/1/hi/business/6096084.stm

292. 'If every last drop of the remaining 1 trillion barrels could be extracted at current cost ratios and current rates of production – which is extremely unlikely – the entire endowment would last only another thirty-seven years.' Kunstler, *The Long Emergency* (2005) 66.

293. Kunstler, *The Long Emergency* (2005) 84.

294. Leeb, *The Coming Economic Collapse* (2006) 77.

295. Klare, *Blood and Oil* (2004) 23.

296. Leeb, *The Coming Economic Collapse* (2006) 22.

297. Leeb, *The Coming Economic Collapse* (2006) 118–19.

298. In the USA, for example, the EIA points out that in 2004 petroleum products contributed about 40.2 per cent of the energy used in the country, compared to 23 per cent for natural gas, 22 per cent for coal and 14 per cent for the combination of nuclear, hydroelectric, geothermal and other sources. 'Apart from transportation fuel, oil is used for home heating. It is a raw material for making plastics, asphalt, and a host of chemical products. Oil is used to make fertilizer for food production and to run farm equipment. And, of course oil provides the energy for manufacturing virtually every product consumers buy.' Leeb, *The Coming Economic Collapse* (2006) 93.

Chapter 16

299. For example, largely invisible to us, a vast slave trade network run by global organised crime has spread its sinister roots. More than 150 countries around the world are either a source, destination, or a transit country for the global slave trade, according to the 2006 *Trafficking in Persons Report*. The most successful crime groups in history run multi-billion dollar empires of drugs, arms dealing, people trafficking and fraud. Annual income from organised crime has passed $2 trillion, a figure higher than the GDP of all countries but the top six economies in the world. So far, our international systems have been powerless to halt the growth of this menace.

300. Bacon, *The Physical and Metaphysical Works including The Advancement of Learning and Novum Organum* (1620) 383.

301. Kant, *Critique of Pure Reason* (1998) (1781) 198.

302. NASA website: http://www.nasa.gov/centers/goddard/about/history/dr_goddard.html.

Appendix 1: Timelines of time

Figure 37: Timeline of the cosmos (13.7 bn years)
and of life (3.5 bn years)

Figure 38: Timeline of humans (300,000 years)

Figure 39: Timeline of civilisations (6,000 years)

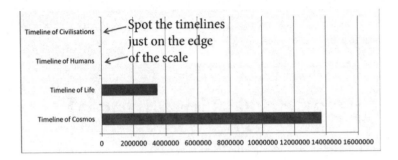

Figure 40 (a): Time perspectives in units of thousands of years

Putting alongside one another the four kinds of time scales shows the pinprick of time occupied in cosmic history by both the lifespan of humans and the lifespan of the enterprise of civilisation:

- Timeline of the cosmos = 13.7 billion years
- Timeline of life = 3.5 billion years
- Timeline of humans = 300,000 years
- Timeline of civilisations = 6,000 years

If we exclude the cosmic timeline, the differences in time scales becomes even more apparent.

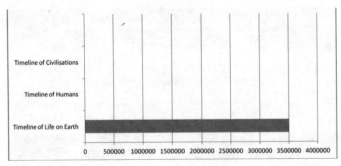

Figure 40 (b): Time perspectives in units of thousands of years

The relevance of these time perspectives for the futurist and the citizen of the future is that they show that human life is still young. The quest for civilisation is only in its infancy. We have made many mistakes in history (too many to mention) but, by way of compensation, we have amassed extraordinary knowledge. Knowledge is the future.

What these timelines also show is that for us the future is far greater than the past. It spans out before us in monumental spans of time.

We have knowledge. We have history as a book of learning. We have science. And we have the future. What excuse can be left if we do not go on to build the greatest civilisations ever seen?

Appendix 2: Trying to imagine a world without oil

It's hard to imagine a world without oil since this incredible substance has been the power behind our industrial and motorised civilisation for well over a century.

First, our huge road transport systems would be effectively paralysed,[1] and, with them, the never-ending supply of 'just-in-time' consumer goods to supermarkets, shopping centres, malls and high-street shops. A huge amount of petroleum is used to keep these transport systems going – the lifelines of our fast-paced, highly mobile societies. Sixty-four per cent of all freight in the USA is moved by truck.[2] Petroleum products account for a massive 97 per cent of all fuel used by America's fleets of cars, trucks, buses, planes, trains and ships.[3] In 2001, America's transportation system alone used 13.5 million barrels of oil per day.[4]

The end of these mass transport systems would shatter in one blow our current retail sector. Big retailers today are dependent upon long-distance haulage and transportation of goods from across the world. The higher costs of a shrinking energy supply will send prices of most retail goods through the roof.

The end of fast long-range transport will also cripple global outsourcing which splits up manufacturing plants from company head offices and branches.

And our car-dependent suburban culture would be instantly dislocated. The greatest demand for petroleum remains, of course, motor gasoline.[5] High oil prices would make long-distance travelling by car a luxury few could afford. We will witness the beginning of the end of our dependence upon cars.

Fuel efficiency is going to be very highly prized in the future. Lubricating oils and greases for automobile engines and other machinery would no longer be available.

Overnight, much of commercial air travel would be suspended and, as a result, the airline business would nosedive: 'It's hard to be optimistic about the future of commercial airlines. Fuel represents about a quarter of their operating costs, but even at 2004 price levels, with fuel supplies still very dependable, the commercial airlines were struggling to stay in business.'[6]

Motorised farming would be severely hampered. With the road transport system on the rack, supplies of coal for powering national electricity power grids will be curtailed, coal being the largest energy source for electricity. This will push up the frequency, and duration, of power cuts.

When the supply of oil runs out, the heating oil that warms up millions of homes across the world every winter would no longer be available. People would have to rely on burning wood for heat and, to a much lesser extent, on electric heaters. The massive demand for wood in the cold Northern Hemisphere will lead to ferocious deforestation. This will exacerbate global warming and environmental degradation.

Since the electricity sector uses 8 per cent of total petroleum consumption, and electric utilities use residual fuel to generate electricity,[7] the production of electricity would also be placed under considerable stress in a world without oil.

And since plastics[8] are derived from natural resources like coal, oil and gas, converting hydrocarbons of these fossil fuels into completely new materials, the manufacture of a vast array of plastic products would be significantly curtailed.

Consumer goods made from plastic, and vital to our daily lives, would no longer be produced on anywhere near the same scale as they are today.[9]

In addition, the production line for mass products made from materials such as nylon, rayon, cellophane, polystyrene, polyester, teflon and polythylene would be largely suspended. There would be no more petroleum jelly used in some medical products and toiletries.

Solvents such as those used in paints, lacquers and printing inks would be in short supply, as would asphalt (used to pave roads and airfields, to surface reservoirs, and to make roofing materials and floor coverings) and petroleum (or paraffin) wax used in candy making, packaging, candles, matches and polishes.

The industrial sector, which is the second largest consumer of petroleum, accounting for about 23 per cent of all petroleum consumption in the USA, would be lost without oil. Distillate fuel oil is used to power diesel engines in buses, trucks, trains, automobiles and other machinery.

What we are seeing here is that the energy crisis will herald the beginning of the end of the Industrial Age. As James Howard Kunstler has said, the decline of oil will lead to the cancellation of the American Dream with its culture of 'extreme car-dependency'.[10] Societies will be forced to downscale to a way of life that will approximate to some sort of Amish lifestyle combined with low-energy technologies.

This is the cold hard truth the modern world is just unable to conceive, let alone accept. That's because no one in the developed world has ever known any other kind of life. No one alive today has any memory of a world without plentiful supplies of cheap oil. The oldest people on the planet now were born into a world already exploding with the mass urbanisation, motorisation and suburbanisation made possible by the Oil Age. We do not know any other world. The collective memories of a hundred years of urbanisation pulse through our blood and our brains.

The final act of the Industrial Age has begun.

Nor is there a great deal of comfort to be found in the contemplation of alternative energy sources, such as coal, gas, wind power, solar energy and nuclear power. None of them alone can support our globalised industrial society: 'Fossil fuels allowed the human race to operate highly complex systems at gigantic scales. Renewable energy sources are not compatible with those systems and scales. Renewables will not be able to take the place of oil and gas in running those systems. The systems themselves will have to go.'[11]

Both solar energy and wind power have nowhere near the capacity required to supply the energy needs of mass urban societies. It is thought that North American coal will peak in the year 2035 and that its gas production has already peaked. As much as 96 per cent of the coal consumed in America is for producing electricity. Clean coal is costly to produce and 'dirty' coal is too risky from a pollution point of view. The biggest single source of global greenhouse gas emissions is the burning of coal to produce electricity. Nuclear power is also very risky in an era of global geopolitical tensions and has significant environmental threats and risks of military deployment associated with it.

The world is running out of ideas, and time, to solve its energy crisis: 'At absolute peak [world oil production], there will still be plenty of oil left in the ground ... but it will be the half that is deeper down, harder and costlier to extract, sitting under harsh and remote parts of the world ... and this remaining oil will be contested by everyone. At peak and beyond, there is massive potential for system failures of all kinds, social, economic, and political... Beyond peak, things unravel and the center does not hold. Beyond peak, all bets are off about civilization's future.'[12]

Already, the energy crisis is well underway. Oil wars have started. Oil prices are escalating. A complex realignment of global and regional power is taking place as control over energy supplies and routes shifts in a fiercely contested environment.

Industrial progress as a concept and as a human ideal is becoming exhausted. We need not just a new word but a new direction.

We need a science of the future to help steer us out of the coming energy crisis and secure a new, more sustainable phase of civilisation.

Notes

1. 'Petroleum products, especially motor gasoline, distillate (diesel) fuel, and jet fuel, provide virtually all of the energy consumed in the transportation sector. Transportation is the greatest single use of petroleum, accounting for an estimated 67 percent of all U.S. petroleum consumed in 2004.' 'Petroleum Products' by the Energy Information Administration (EIA) – http://www.eia.doe.gov (official energy statistics from the US Govt), September 2005.

2. Kunstler, *The Long Emergency* (2005) 264.

3. Klare, *Blood and Oil* (2004) 7.

4. Klare, *Blood and Oil* (2004) 17.

5. 'Petroleum Products' – EIA, September 2005 (more information on this subject can be found in the following EIA publication: 'Petroleum: An Energy Profile').

6. Kunstler, *The Long Emergency* (2005) 270.

7. Distillate fuel oil is used to heat residential and commercial buildings and to fire industrial and electric utility boilers.

8. The American Plastics Council estimates that there are no fewer than 10,000 different kinds of plastic. 'What is Plastic?' – The American Plastics Council – www.plastics.org. With plastics, which never decompose completely, you have a synthetic material made from non-renewable natural resources, like petroleum and/or natural gas, and which has been made into a non-biodegradable product – a 'double whammy' for environmentalism.

9. We are talking about toys, kitchenware, plastic packets, some stationery items, domestic and garden utensils, types of furniture, cool-drink bottles, plastic bank cards, velcro fastening systems, CD-roms, plastic cups, plugs, trinkets, acrylics, microwave cookware, babies' bottles, black garbage bags, straws, nappies, contact lenses and syringes. As products like these would no longer be widely available, more costly alternative materials would suddenly be required on a massive scale.

10. Kunstler, *The Long Emergency* (2005) 283. In 1900, most Americans still lived on farms and the country's culture was impregnated with rural values. Even in the 1920s, 30 per cent of the population lived on farms. Motorization changed all that. Car ownership in the country rose from 1.8 million to 9.2 million between 1914 and 1920,with annual car production by 1923 reaching 3.5 million. In 1955 the US government decided to build its colossal inter-state highway, an amazing public works project of pyramidal proportions. By 1974, 85 per cent of Americans drove to work every day. So the USA transformed itself in the first 74 years of the twentieth century from a rural population into a car-dependent suburban population. As America's car culture grew, so the rural life based on horses declined. There were 21 million horses in the USA in 1915 – their population has shrunk to 7 million today, with about 725,000 used for racing (see Kunstler, *The Long Emergency* (2005) 245).

11. Kunstler, *The Long Emergency* (2005) 131.

12. Kunstler, *The Long Emergency* (2005) 65.

References

Aldrin, B. 2013. *Mission to Mars*. Washington, D.C.: National Geographic.

Aquinas, T. 2003 (1265–74). *A Summary of Philosophy*. Indianapolis: Hackett Publishing Company.

Aristotle. 2008 (350 BC). *Physics*. Oxford: Oxford University Press.

Bacon, F. (1620). *The Physical and Metaphysical Works: Including the Advancement of Learning and Novum Organum*. Marston Gate: Amazon.

Eds Beebee, H. , Hitchcock, C. & Menzies, P. 2009. *The Oxford Handbook of Causation*. Oxford: Oxford University Press.

Bodanis, D. 2000. *E=mc²*. New York: Berkeley Books.

Brown, C.S. 2007. *Big History: from the Big Bang to the Present*. New York: The New Press.

Buchanan, P. J. 2002. *The Death of the West*. New York: Thomas Dunne Books.

Capra, F. 1996. *The Web of Life*. London: Flamingo.

Clark, K. 1969. *Civilisation*. London: John Murray.

Concise Routledge Encyclopedia of Philosophy. 2000. London: Routledge.

Copernicus, N. 1995 (1543). *On the Revolutions of Heavenly Spheres*. New York: Prometheus Books.

Cox, B. & Forshaw, J. 2009. *Why does E=mc²?* Cambridge, MA: Da Capo Press.

Ed. Crystal, D. 2000. *The Cambridge Encyclopedia* (Fourth Edition). Cambridge: Cambridge University Press.

Dacke, M., Baird, E., Byrne, M., Clarke H. & Scholtz, E. 2013. 'Dung Beetles Use the Milky Way for Orientation'. *Current Biology*. Volume 23, Issue 4, 18 February 2013, Pages 298–300.

De Caritat, J.A.N (Marquis de Condorcet). 1795. *Outlines of an historical view of the progress of the human mind*. Moscow: Book Renaissance.

Dent, H. 2011. *The Great Crash Ahead*. New York: Free Press.

Descartes, R. (1637). 1999. *Discourse on Method for Guiding Reason and Searching for Truth in the Sciences and Related Writings*. London: Penguin Books.

Descartes, R. (1641). 1998. *Meditations and Other Metaphysical Writings*. London: Penguin Books.

Ed. Dyke, H. & Bardon, A. 2013. *A Companion to the Philosophy of Time*. Chichester: John Wiley & Sons.

Einstein, A. 1916. *Relativity*. St Petersburg, Florida: Red and Black Publishers.

Einstein, A. 1931. *The World as I See It*. New York: The Wisdom Library.

Einstein, A. Foreword to Galilei, Galileo. 2001 (1632). *Dialogue Concerning the Two Chief World Systems*. New York: The Modern Library.

Euclid. 2013 (c. 300 BC). *Elements*. New Mexico: Green Lion Press.

Ferguson, N. 2012. *The Great Degeneration: How Institutions and Economies Die*. London: Penguin Books.

Fuller, B.R. 1969. *Operating Manual for Spaceship Earth*. Zurich: Lars Muller Publishers.

Galbraith, J.K. 1987. *A History of Economics – The Past as the Present*. London: Penguin.

Galbraith, J.K. 1954. *The Great Crash 1929*. London: Penguin.

Galilei, Galileo. 2001 (1632). *Dialogue Concerning the Two Chief World Systems*. New York: The Modern Library.

Galilei, Galileo. 2012. *Selected Writings.* Oxford: Oxford University Press.

Gleick, J. *Chaos: Making a New Science.* 1987. New York: Viking.

Hacking, I. 2001. *An Introduction to Probability and Inductive Logic.* Cambridge: Cambridge University Press.

Hawking, S. 2005. *God Created the Integers.* London: Penguin Books.

Hawking, S. 2002. *On the Shoulders of Giants.* London: Running Press.

Hawking, S. 2008. *Stephen Hawking and the Theory of Everything* (Channel 4 and Discovery TV documentary).

Hawking, S. & Mlodinow, L. 2010. *The Grand Design.* London: Bantam Press.

Hegel, G.W.F. 1990. *Encyclopedia of the Philosophical Sciences in Outline and Critical Writings.* New York: Continuum.

Hegel, G.W.F. 1977 (1807). *Phenomenology of Spirit.* Oxford: Oxford University Press.

Hume, D. 2008 (1748). *An Enquiry concerning Human Understanding.* Oxford: Oxford University Press.

Hume, D. 1985 (1739–40). *A Treatise of Human Nature.* London: Penguin Classics.

Hume, D. 2008 (1779). *Dialogues Concerning Natural Religion* and *Natural History of Religion.* Oxford: Oxford University Press.

Jackson, T. 2012. *The Elements: An Illustrated History of the Periodic Table.* New York: Shelter Harbor Press.

Kant, I. 1998 (1781). *Critique of Pure Reason.* London: Everyman.

Kennedy, J.F. 1962. *Address on the First Anniversary of the Alliance for Progress.* Public Papers of the Presidents. http://www.presidency.ucsb.edu/ws/?pid=9100

Kepler, J. 2008 (1619). *Harmonies of the World*. London: Forgotten Books.

Keynes, J.M. 1920. *A Treatise on Probability*. London: Macmillan & Co.

Klare, M. 2004. *Blood and Oil*. London: Penguin Books.

Kondratieff, N. 1935. *The Long Waves in Economic Life*. Whitefish, MT: Kessinger Publishing's Legacy Reprints.

Kunstler, J.H. 2005. *The Long Emergency*. New York: Grove Press.

Laplace, Pierre-Simon. 1814. *A Philosophical Essay on Probabilities*. New York: John Wiley & Sons.

Laplace, Pierre-Simon. 1822. *A Treatise of Celestial Mechanics*. London: BiblioLife.

Lee, M. 2012. *Knowing our Future – the startling case for futurology*. Oxford: Infinite Ideas.

Leeb, S. 2006. *The Coming Economic Collapse*. New York: Warner Business Books.

Longman, P. 2004. *The Empty Cradle*. New York: Basic Books.

Magnus, G. 2009. *The Age of Ageing*. Singapore: John Wiley & Sons (Asia).

Mandela, N.R. 1994. *Long Walk to Freedom*. London: Little, Brown.

Mellor, D.H. 1995. *The Facts of Causation*. London & New York: Routledge.

Mitchell, M. 2009. *Complexity: A Guided Tour*. Oxford: Oxford University Press.

Mlodinow, L. 2008. *The Drunkard's Walk: how randomness rules our lives*. London: Penguin Books.

Moore, H.L. 1914. *Economic Cycles: their Law and Cause*. New York: The Macmillan Company.

Morris, I. 2011. *Why the West Rules – For Now – The Patterns of History and What They Reveal about the Future*. London: Profile Books.

Newton, I. 1995 (1687). *The Principia*. New York: Prometheus Books.

Oaklander, L.N. 2004. *The Ontology of Time*. New York: Prometheus Books.

Orzel, C. 2012. *How to teach relativity to your dog*. New York: Basic Books.

Paul, L.A. & and Hall, N. 2013. *Causation: A User's Guide*. Oxford: Oxford University Press.

Ed. Pearsall, J. 1998. *The New Oxford Dictionary of English*. Oxford: Oxford University Press.

Poincaré, H. 1913. *The Foundations of Science*. Marston Gate: Amazon.

Prestowitz, C. 2005. *Three Billion New Capitalists – the great shift of wealth and power to the East*. New York: Basic Books.

Prigogine, I. 1996. *The End of Certainty*. New York: The Free Press.

Psillos, S. 2002. *Causation and Explanation*. Durham: Acumen.

Reichenbach, H. 1956. *The Direction of Time*. New York: Dover Publications.

Reichenbach, H. 1958. *The Philosophy of Space and Time*. New York: Dover Publications.

Reichenbach, H. 1951. *The Rise of Scientific Philosophy*. Berkeley: University of California Press

Richeson, D. 2008. *Euler's Gem – the polyhedron formula and the birth of topology*. Princeton: Princeton University Press.

Ridley, M. 1999. *Genome: the Autobiography of a Species in 23 Chapters*. London: Harper Perennial.

Russell, B. 1996 (1946). *History of Western Philosophy*. London & New York: Routledge Classics.

Schumpeter, J. 1939. *Business Cycles – A Theoretical, Historical and Statistical Analysis of the Capitalist Process*. Chevy Chase, MD: Bartleby's Books.

Schumpeter, J. 1934. *The Theory of Economic Development.* New Brunswick: Transaction Publishers.

Eds Simpson, R.D., Toman, M.A. & Ayres, R. 2005. *Scarcity and Growth Revisited.* Washington: Resources for the Future.

Sorokin, P. 1957. *Social and Cultural Dynamics.* Boston: Porter Sargent Publisher.

Spier, F. 2011. *Big History and the Future of Humanity.* Chichester: Wiley-Blackwell.

Strogatz, S. 2003. *Sync: the emerging science of spontaneous order.* London: Penguin.

Toynbee, A.J. 1946. *A Study of History* Volumes 1–V1. Oxford: Oxford University Press.

Toynbee, A.J. 1957. *A Study of History* Volumes V11–X. Oxford: Oxford University Press.

Van der Heijden, K. 2005. *Scenarios – the Art of Strategic Conversation* (Second Edition). Chichester: John Wiley & Sons.

Weinert, F. 2013. *The March of Time.* London: Springer.

Winfree, A. 1987. *The Timing of Biological Clocks.* New York: Scientific American Books, Inc.

Wolfram, S. 2002. *A New Kind of Science.* Champaign, IL: Wolfram Media, Inc.

Websites

American Plastics Council – www.plastics.org

BBC news – http://news.bbc.co.uk:

'Divorce rate highest since 1996', BBC News – UK Edition, 31 August 2005

'Domestic abusers face crackdown', BBC News.com, 3 December 2003

'Climate resets "Doomsday Clock"', by Molly Bentley, 17 January 2007

'Climate change fight can't wait', BBC.News.com, 31 October 2006

Civitas – www.civitas.org

Centre for Research on the Epidemiology of Disasters – www.cred.be

Divorce Magazine – www.DivorceMagazine.com

Energy Information Administration – www.eia.doe.gov

Institute of Futurology – www.futurology.co.za

National Coalition Against Domestic Violence – www.ncadv.org

Refuge – www.refuge.org.uk

Suicide Reference Library – www.suicidereferencelibrary.com

University College London (UCL), see Global Drought Monitor – www.ucl.ac.uk

United Nations, see 'The Future We Want' and 'Millennium Ecosystem Assessment' (2005) – www.un.org/en/sustainablefuture

Stephen Wolfram – www.wolfram.com

Index

Speaking across borders:
the role of higher education
in furthering intercultural dialogue

Sjur Bergan and Hilligje van't Land (eds)

Council of Europe Publishing

This publication has been edited jointly by the Council of Europe and the International Association of Universities (www.iau-aiu.net).

Cover illustration: © Shutterstock

Cover design: Documents and Publications Production Department (SPDP), Council of Europe

Layout: Jouve, Paris

Council of Europe Publishing
F-67075 Strasbourg Cedex
http://book.coe.int

ISBN 978-92-871-6941-9
© Council of Europe, November 2010
Printed at the Council of Europe